Worcestershire
MURDERS

NICOLA SLY

The
History
Press

ALSO BY THE AUTHOR

Bristol Murders
Cornish Murders (with John Van der Kiste)
Dorset Murders
Hampshire Murders
Shropshire Murders
Somerset Murders (with John Van der Kiste)
Wiltshire Murders

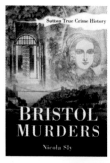
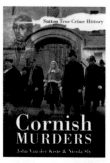

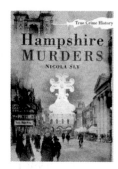

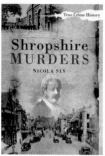
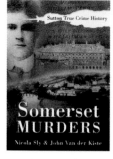
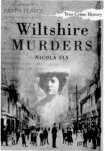

First published 2009

The History Press
The Mill, Brimscombe Port
Stroud, Gloucestershire, GL5 2QG
www.thehistorypress.co.uk

British Library Cataloguing in Publication Data.
A catalogue record for this book is available from the British Library.

ISBN 978 0 7524 4898 5

Typesetting and origination by The History Press
Printed in Great Britain

CONTENTS

AUTHOR'S NOTE & ACKNOWLEDGEMENTS

aving been married for almost twenty years to a man who was born and raised in Kidderminster, I was only too pleased to be asked to compile *Worcestershire Murders*. However, while researching this collection of true cases, it quickly became evident that the county boundaries of Worcestershire have, over the years, been somewhat fluid. I came across one man who, without moving house, had actually lived in three different counties, and there were also places like Dudley, which historically was an isolated 'island' of Worcestershire, geographically located in the county of Staffordshire. Hence, I made the decision to include those cases for which the location was given as Worcestershire at the time of the murder.

As with any other county, historically there are those in Worcestershire to whom human life means very little. These include people who killed purely for financial gain, such as William Lightband who murdered elderly shopkeeper Joseph Hawkins at Areley Kings in 1836, and the band of wealthy landowners who arranged the murder of the rector of Oddingley in 1806 to avoid paying what they considered to be unfair tithes, then murdered the killer they hired to ensure that their villainy would never be revealed.

Others killed through jealousy, such as William Yarnold who murdered his estranged wife in Worcester in 1925. Some turned to murder simply to rid themselves of a person who had become a perceived nuisance, as in the case of Charles Wall who callously threw his fiancée's five-year-old daughter down a mineshaft at Old Swinford in 1830.

Some murders remain unsolved to this day, such as those of Florrie Porter at Lickey End, near Bromsgrove, in 1944 and Patrick Mulligan, murdered in Worcester in 1961. Yet perhaps the biggest mystery of all surrounds 'Hagley Bella', whose body was found wedged in a hollow tree in 1943 – not only has her killer never been identified, but also, in this case, neither has the victim.

As always, there are numerous people to be acknowledged and thanked. John J. Eddleston and Steve Fielding have both previously published reference books, which

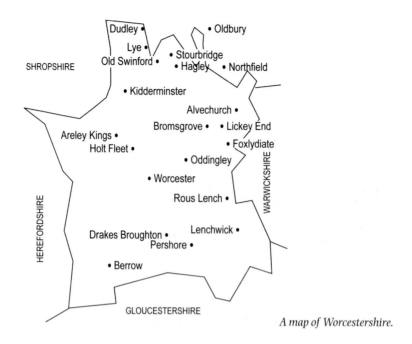

A map of Worcestershire.

contain a mine of information on British murders and executions. Anne Bradford has written a fascinating book on murder in and around Worcester, and Donald McCormick penned an intriguing book on the case of 'Hagley Bella'. These books are recorded in more detail in the bibliography, as are the local and national newspapers from which the details of the featured cases were drawn. I am especially grateful to the *Express and Star*, Wolverhampton, for permission to use pictures pertaining to the Hagley Bella case, to the *Worcester News* for allowing me to use their picture of Florrie Porter and also to the BBC at Birmingham for supplying me with a DVD of their *Inside Out* programme, which covered her murder. My thanks must also go to the staff of the Worcestershire Archives for their help with my research, and particularly with their assistance in helping me to unravel the numerous county boundary changes over the years. The retired policeman from Stourbridge, who shared his observations on some of the more recent cases featured, wished to remain anonymous, but nevertheless his contributions were very much appreciated.

On a more personal level, John Van der Kiste was, as always, generous with his help and advice. My grateful thanks also go to my brother-in-law and sister-in-law, John and Sue, who opened their home to us during our visits to Worcestershire. My husband Richard's local knowledge of the area proved invaluable and, as usual, he acted as chauffeur on my research and photography trips. As always, Richard generously proofread every word of this book and invariably improved the content with his observations. My father, John Higginson, remains my inspiration.

Finally, my thanks must go to Matilda Richards, my editor at The History Press, for her continued help and encouragement.

1

'THE GIRL LOOKS JUST THE SAME AS SHE DID WHEN SHE WAS ASLEEP'

Berrow, 1780

In the early hours of the morning of 7 May 1780, Mr Player, a cottager from Berrow, was awakened from his sleep by a terrible howling noise coming from the direction of his neighbour's home. Player shook his wife awake and together they listened intently for a few moments, hearing the howls repeated, closely followed by a loud thumping sound, as if something heavy had fallen onto a wooden floor.

Courageously, Mr Player got up and went to investigate the dreadful noises. The front door to his neighbour's cottage was tightly closed, but Player could hear sounds coming from within. He shouted several times for his neighbour, Edward Gummary, but received no reply so he eventually walked round to the back of the cottage. The back door was also closed, but Player could hear someone moving about in the kitchen. Assuming that it was Edward's wife, Elizabeth, Player called out to her, but again received no response.

Concerned, he ran back to his own cottage and roused his wife, telling her that there appeared to be something dreadfully wrong at the Gummary's home. Mrs Player accompanied her husband back to their neighbour's cottage, where now the front door stood wide open. To their horror, the Players could see blood dripping through the kitchen ceiling from the bedroom above. Mr Player immediately rushed upstairs, where a scene of terrible carnage awaited him.

Two dead bodies lay on the floor of the bedroom, close to the bed. The sight so upset Mr Player that he found himself unable to check on the other occupants of the house. Instead, he and his wife rushed to summon assistance from neighbours.

When somebody finally had the stomach to investigate the Gummary's cottage more closely, they found that one of the bodies on the bedroom floor was that of Edward Gummary. He had a large wound between his collarbone and his neck, which had penetrated his chest and almost severed his arm from his body. He had numerous other injuries, including cuts to his head and face, a deep wound below his ribcage through which parts of his bowel protruded, a leg wound with a broken fibula, and several deep cuts to his hands, which suggested that he had fought desperately with his attackers. Close by lay his wife, with wounds to her face and head that were deep enough to expose her brain. Her nose had been completely chopped from her face.

Actually in the bed was the body of the Gummary's nine-year-old daughter, Ann. A deep wound to the side of her neck had severed both her jugular artery and her spine. Finally, in a neighbouring bedroom, a visitor to the house lay dead. Elizabeth Gummary's brother, Thomas Sheen, had serious wounds to his head and chest.

All of the bodies were dressed in their nightclothes and, it seemed, had been savagely attacked by someone frenziedly wielding a weapon, such as an axe, while they lay sleeping peacefully in their beds.

The alarm was raised immediately and neighbours quickly launched a hunt for any strangers in the area. In a field about a quarter of a mile from the Gummary's house, six gypsies were rounded up and handed over to the authorities, although there was no real evidence to connect any one of them with the slaughter of the entire Gummary family. A young child who was with the travelling families tearfully told the villagers, 'It was not my daddy that killed them, but two men who are gone to Tewkesbury.'

One of the gypsies had a small amount of blood on his clothing and a bloody stick was found in his possession. Taken back to the scene of the crime, he was alleged to have said, 'The girl looks just the same as she did when she was asleep.' However, it was apparent that, given the extent of the massacre within the house, any man who had been involved would have had more than a small amount of blood on his person and eventually the gypsy families were released without charge.

An inquest was opened before coroner Harry Long and a verdict of 'wilful murder by person or persons unknown' was recorded on all four victims. The bodies were buried on 11 May 1780 in Berrow churchyard, their final resting place later marked with a memorial plaque on the outside wall of the church.

There were no clues to the identity of the assailant or assailants and indeed, it was impossible to even suggest a motive for the brutal murders of the entire family. None of the victims was known to have any enemies, or to have recently quarrelled with anybody. The cottage showed no signs of having been ransacked and considerable sums of money were found untouched. A total of 29s 8d in coins was found in the cottage, in addition to 3s 6d farthing in the pockets of Thomas Sheen, and it was generally agreed that this was about the correct amount that should have been in the possession of the deceased family, meaning that theft was not a motive for their slaughter.

With no conceivable motive, no clues and absolutely no evidence, it seemed as if whoever had killed the Gummary family had literally got away with murder. Two men, William Jones and William Addis, who had been caught destroying the nearby Malvern Link fence, were strongly suspected of being the murderers at the time but, since there was no concrete evidence against them, they could only be charged with destroying the fence, for which both were imprisoned.

In fact, it was to be almost thirty years before a possible clue to the identity of the killer or killers emerged. In January 1809, an eighty-year-old man was admitted to the Worcester Royal Infirmary with a broken leg. Delirious with pain, James Traynton began to talk. Another patient heard his ramblings and immediately recognised what he believed to be details of the murder of the Gummary family, so many years earlier.

When questioned directly, Traynton seemed to have some knowledge of the murders, although he would only admit to helping to destroy the fence, holding a ladder against the window and supplying the murderers with drink. He assured nurses that all the murderers were still alive and of a similar age to himself, telling them that the murders had been committed using 'bills'. (A 'bill' is a shortened name for a billhook, a sharp, long-bladed hatchet used for hedge trimming.) In between talking about the murders, Traynton raved about being pursued by demons, judged by his fellow patients as being the signs of a guilty conscience.

The memorial stone for the Gummary family in Berrow churchyard. (© N. Sly, 2008)

Traynton died four days after his admission to hospital, unfortunately without naming any of the alleged murderers of the Gummary family. It was established after his death that he had once worked as a labourer on the Malvern Link enclosure and had, in the past, been thought of as a 'bad character'.

Whether or not Traynton's demented ramblings betrayed his involvement in the slaying of an entire family will now never be known and officially the case remains unsolved.

Note: In some accounts the family name is given as Gummery. I have used the spelling shown on the memorial stone although, of course, there is no guarantee that the mason was correct in his interpretation.

2

'WHAT IS TO BE DONE WITH HIM NOW?'

Oddingley, 1806 and 1830

On 24 June 1806, Thomas Giles and John Lench were walking along a lane near Oddingley when they heard the report of a gun, followed by a shout of 'Murder!' The two men rushed to investigate and soon came across a man skulking in the hedgerow, a bag in his hand.

'Villain, what have you been doing?' the men asked him.

'Me? Nothing,' replied the man, dropping his bag and running off.

A few yards further along the lane, the two men became aware of something burning on the ground. When they got closer, they realised that it was in fact a man who had obviously been shot and whose clothes were now on fire.

Lench began to pull the man's burning clothes from his body and, once he was sure that all the flames had been extinguished, he set off in pursuit of the man who had just fled. Meanwhile, Giles ran to the nearest house to summon help. That house turned out to be the vicarage and a servant there sent for the rector of the next parish, Reginald Pynder, who was at that time also acting as a County Magistrate. Pynder immediately saddled his horse and galloped to where the badly injured man lay, and, on his arrival, he was surprised to find that the victim of the shooting was Revd George Parker, the rector of the parish of Oddingley. Sadly, Parker died within minutes of Pynder's arrival.

It was apparent from Parker's injuries that his assailant had first shot him, the ball penetrating his right side. Seeing that his victim was still alive, the gunman had then clubbed him over the head with the butt of his gun, which had broken, leaving Revd Parker with two large cuts over his left eye. Finally, he had set his victim on fire, at which point he had been interrupted by the unexpected arrival of Giles and Lench.

The bag that the attacker had dropped was found to contain the pieces of a broken gun. Soon, John Lench returned from his pursuit of the murderer to say that he had almost caught up with him when the man had put his hand in his pocket as if to withdraw a pistol and threatened to shoot Lench if he came any nearer. Wisely, Lench backed off, leaving his quarry to escape across the fields.

Giles and Lench described the attacker as being about 5ft 5in tall, with dark brown hair, balding at the front. A black beard framed his face and he was wearing a long, blue coat with metal buttons. This sounded to the police very much like a description of Richard Hemming from Oddingley, who, although he worked legitimately as a carpenter, was known locally as a shady character, whom the police suspected of being responsible for several robberies in the area.

By the time the police got to Hemming's home, he was nowhere to be found. Enquiries revealed that he had been seen heading towards Worcester on the afternoon of Parker's murder and he was later seen at a public house. There was one more alleged sighting of him a week later, when a girl told police that she believed that she had seen him running into a wood. However, the police never managed to catch Richard Hemming who, it seemed, had disappeared without a trace, leaving his wife and three young children behind. Even if he was a man of suspicious character, Elizabeth Hemming swore that Richard was a loving husband and father and insisted that he would never have left without telling her.

An inquest was opened into Parker's murder on the following day, at which the foreman of the coroner's jury was a man named Captain Evans. There were later to be allegations of malpractice at the inquest, with some evidence not being presented and the proceedings being rushed in order to conclude them within the day. However, the jury eventually returned a verdict of 'murder against some person or persons at present unknown'.

There were so many complaints about the inquest that the county magistrates felt obliged to hold an investigation. As foreman of the jury, Captain Evans, was interviewed and told the magistrates that he was so keen to see Parker's murderer apprehended that he was personally starting a fund to provide a reward for anyone with information about the killer. This so impressed the magistrates that they immediately offered a donation of £50 towards the fund.

Since the only viable suspect in the murder of Revd Parker seemed to have vanished off the face of the earth, the police found themselves at a standstill with their investigations and the case went cold. It was not until 1830 that it was revived, after the discovery of a body at Netherwood Farm in the village.

At that time, a barn at the farm was in a bad state of repair and the tenants asked their landlord, Mr Galton, if they might demolish it. Galton agreed and the Waterson family engaged the services of a local labourer, Charles Burton, to carry out the demolition. Burton began work on 21 January 1830 and, while digging round the barn's foundations, he discovered an old boot buried in the ground, a skeletal foot still in it. His next shovel-full of earth contained a second boot and foot; Burton stopped digging and notified the police.

The earth around the barn's foundations was loose and, when the police dug down to a depth of 18in, they uncovered the complete skeleton of a man, lying on his left side. The man's skull was cracked and his upper and lower jaws were broken. As well as the man's remains, the police also excavated the remnants of a woollen waistcoat and some cord trousers. Various personal effects were buried with the man, including a few coins, a whetstone, a clasp knife and a carpenter's slide rule.

As the wife of the only man known to be missing in the area, Elizabeth Hemming was called to view these items and identified the boots and the rule as being the property of her husband, Richard. She recalled a crack in the rule where it had once been dropped and recognised the boots by their turned up toes and by nails in the heels. (Coincidentally, labourer Charles Burton was Elizabeth's brother.)

At the time that Hemming had disappeared, Thomas Clewes had owned Netherwood Farm and he was promptly arrested on suspicion of his murder. Coroner Mr Smith opened an inquest at the Talbot Inn into Hemming's death and, on the third day of the proceedings, Clewes' gaoler passed a message to the coroner saying that Clewes wished to make a statement.

Revd Parker had been a kindly man, who was always willing to help any of his parishioners who might be in need. That said, he was not a popular man, as he was also extremely parsimonious and was a stickler for collecting the biggest possible tithes from the wealthier villagers.

Parker's position as rector was unsalaried and thus he survived solely on the annual tithes that he collected. These were normally a tenth of any produce or stock held by landowners each year and were payable either in goods or in cash. The payment of the tithes had long been disputed by the landowners of Oddingley and, when Revd Parker took over as rector of the parish, he apparently became a little greedy and insisted that the landowners paid their dues in kind.

The average tithes paid by each landowner was £30 a year, but as a result of the war in France, the price of goods rocketed, meaning that, by paying in kind, the landowners were paying much more than the amount they might reasonably have expected to pay. As a group, they approached the Revd Parker asking if they might pay in cash instead, even offering to increase their cash payments to £70 a year, but Parker refused. He added insult to injury by trying to insist that, since the landowners were paying him with goods, it was their responsibility to buy him a barn at a cost of £150, in which to keep the animals and store the grain with which they were paying him. The last straw for the farmers was when Revd Parker then complained bitterly about the cost of the dinners that the men regularly held at a nearby pub, the God Speed the Plough Inn.

Clewes told the inquest that he and five other men had got together and made a decision that something must be done about the situation. The leader of the breakaway group was Captain Evans – the man who had served as foreman of the jury at the inquest into Parker's death – and he was joined in his scheming by Clewes, John Barnett, Joseph Taylor and brothers William and George Banks.

As prominent citizens, it was obviously impossible for the conspirators to be directly implicated in Parker's death themselves, hence Richard Hemming was hired for the sum of £50 to kill the rector and provided with a gun by Captain Evans. However, once the deed was done and Evans and his cohorts realised that Hemming had been seen, they found themselves in a quandary. If Hemming were arrested for the murder, then he would surely try to save his own skin by telling the authorities who it was in the village that had wanted Parker dead.

Hemming was told to hide himself in Thomas Clewes' barn while a plan was hatched for his escape. At eleven o'clock on the night after the murder, Evans, Taylor and George Banks called at Clewes' home and the four men went out to the barn, where Richard Hemming had concealed himself under some loose straw. Evans called out to Hemming, telling him that he had brought some food for him. As Hemming wriggled out from under the straw, Joseph Taylor, the village blacksmith, stepped forward and hit him two or three times over the head with his blood stick. (A blood stick was a piece of hard wood, loaded at one end with lead and resembling a small mallet in appearance, used when bleeding horses, to strike a blade into a vein.)

Clewes professed himself to have been appalled at this, saying that it had been his belief that Hemming was to be given money and helped to escape. Had he known what was actually going to happen, said Clewes, he would never have gone to the barn. However, there was no time for recriminations as the men now had a dead body on their hands and a pressing need to dispose of it. 'What is to be done with him now?' asked Taylor.

Captain Evans supervised the digging of a hole near the outside wall of the barn then he and Taylor unceremoniously dragged Hemming's body outside and buried it in the hole. The entire process took less than thirty minutes.

Clewes' statement continued, describing the day after Hemming's death on which Clewes had gone to Pershore Fair. While at the fair, George Banks and John Barnett had approached him and both men had given him a package of money totalling around £27, saying that it was his share of the money that had been intended for Richard Hemming, to help him escape. 'Be sure you never split,' Barnett warned Clewes.

For the next few years, the landowners did everything in their power to keep Clewes sweet. He was advanced a large loan without any security and was also given a black mare by Captain Evans – having bid for it at a farm sale, the mare was knocked down to Clewes and Evans later picked up the £22 bill.

As a result of Clewes' statement at the inquest, the police immediately sought the remaining landowners, prepared to arrest them for their part in the murders of George Parker and Richard Hemming.

Twenty-four years had passed since the murders and Captain Evans and Joseph Taylor – the two alleged murderers of Richard Hemming – had both since died. Captain Evans had lived to the age of ninety-five, dying in May 1829. For the last few years of his life, he had drunk a bottle of brandy a day and had been tormented by terrible hallucinations, which appeared to those who witnessed them as if a ghost were haunting him.

The police charged the surviving members of the group – Thomas Clewes, John Barnett and George Banks – with being accessories after the facts of the murders of both Richard Hemming and George Parker. Thomas Clewes alone was additionally charged with the murder of Richard Hemming, with having aided and abetted Taylor in striking him and with harbouring the murderer of George Parker. The three defendants stood trial together at the Spring Assizes in Worcester before Mr Justice Littledale.

The first half of the trial consisted mainly of arguments put by the counsels for the defence on the legalities of the charges against their clients. All three men had retained separate counsels and all three counsels disputed the legality of trying men as accessories after the fact in a murder case when the actual murderer had not been tried. They maintained that, unless someone had been tried and convicted of committing a murder, in the eyes of the law, no murder had actually been proven. Eventually, Barnett and Banks were temporarily discharged and the trial proceeded with Clewes as the only defendant, charged with the wilful murder of Richard Hemming. Clewes pleaded 'Not Guilty'.

The court then heard from a number of witnesses including Charles Burton, Elizabeth Hemming (who had since remarried and was now Elizabeth Newbury) and surgeon, Matthew Pierpoint, who had examined the remains of Richard Hemming. Then those people who had been involved in the aftermath of the murder of George Parker were called, including John Lench, who had found the body (Thomas Giles having since died), Daniel Cole, who had performed the post-mortem examination, and the police who had been involved in the search for Hemming after Parker's murder. A handful of villagers who believed that they could connect Parker's murder with Hemming testified, including John Perkins who had seen Hemming waiting for Parker to pass by on the day of the murder and had also seen him drinking with Thomas Clewes, six weeks prior to Parker's death.

Despite the objections of Clewes' defence counsel, his statement to the coroner was read out in court, in which he confessed to witnessing the murder of Hemming. The confession had been made to magistrate Revd Clifton and he too was called to court to be interrogated. Clifton admitted that he had initially told Clewes that he would make every effort to prevent any personal ill consequences falling on him as a result of giving his statement. After taking the statement, Clifton had immediately become worried about making this promise and had even written to the Secretary of State for advice. When he received a reply from the Under Secretary, he told the court that he had gone back to Clewes and told him that he was unable to guarantee his original promise.

Clifton told Clewes that he had told no one what he had said and that, if Clewes wanted, the matter could be forgotten. However, Clewes had insisted that his statement was put before the coroner regardless.

It finally fell to the judge to sum up the long, complicated case for the jury, which he did at great length. He warned them that they must reach their verdict only on the evidence that they had heard in court that day. He told them that they had heard evidence on Parker's murder only because it seemed to be the precursor of Hemming's murder, which was the case under consideration. Telling the jury that Clewes' confession was the only real evidence against him, he passed an opinion that the confession implicated Clewes as an accessory after the fact but that, as far as he could see, the killing of Hemming seemed to have been done without Clewes' participation. There was no evidence that he had concealed Hemming after Parker's murder and the only evidence that Captain Evans and Taylor were responsible for killing Hemming was Clewes' confession.

To be an accessory to murder in the eyes of the law, Clewes did not have to have struck the final blow but need only have encouraged the act or participated in the killing in any way. Mr Justice Littledale believed that the confession suggested that he had done neither.

The jury retired briefly before returning with a verdict of 'Guilty as an accessory after the fact'. However, when the judge reminded them that the charge against Clewes was actually one of murder, they immediately acquitted him. On his acquittal, the counsel for the prosecution told the court that they did not intend to proceed with their case against John Barnett and George Banks.

All three defendants were discharged from the court and on their return to Oddingley a big party was thrown in their honour. Thomas Clewes later took over as the landlord of the Fir Tree Inn at nearby Dunhampstead, where he displayed press reports about the murders on the walls. The 'Murderer's Bar' is still in existence today. Meanwhile, the village pub in Tibberton, where the plot to murder Revd Parker was allegedly hatched, was ordered to change its name from God Speed the Plough to Speed the Plough in view of the godless act perpetrated within its walls.

Note: As might be expected in a case that occurred so long ago, there are some discrepancies in the contemporary newspaper accounts. Richard Hemming's name is alternately spelled Heming or Hemings. The name Banks is also spelled Bankes and Taylor is alternatively named Joseph and James. Pynder's name is sometimes spelled Pinder.

3

'WHY DIDST THOU LEAVE ME?'

Lye Waste, 1829

On Saturday 29 August 1829, mine surveyor Thomas Higgs was walking past a pit in the Haye Dingle, near Lye Waste in the parish of Old Swinford, when something white caught his eye. After staring at the white object for a few moments, he realised that he was actually looking at a human body, which lay face up in a couple of inches of water at the bottom of the pit.

The sides of the pit, which was about 18 yards deep, were steep and sheer and it was obvious to Higgs that he would be unable to reach the body without ropes. He rushed to fetch miner William Cartwright, who came to the pit with his brother, James. William was roped and Higgs and James lowered him carefully to the pit bottom, where he found the body of a woman lying on her back. Between them the three men managed to haul the dead woman from the depths of the pit and carried her to the Swan Inn at Lye Waste.

On the following morning surgeon William Freer from Stourbridge was called to perform a post-mortem examination on the body. He found that the woman had a fractured hip but, surprisingly, no bruises anywhere on her body. At the back of her head were two large, rough cuts that were full of grit. Working in a mining area, Freer had seen this particular kind of wound numerous times and was able to state with confidence that the injuries to the back of the woman's head had been caused by her fall into the pit. However, the woman had another wound on her right eye and the cause of that injury was much more difficult for the surgeon to determine.

He was hampered by the fact that maggots had eaten away at the edges of the wound. The eye itself had been knocked out and the surgeon believed that this injury had not resulted from the woman's fall. Had it occurred when she fell, Freer would have expected to observe abrasions to the surrounding skin, the presence of grit in the wound and also some damage to the more prominent orbital bone above the eyebrow. Thus, although he was unable to say what had caused the wound, he was fairly certain that it had occurred before she fell. There were no corresponding skull fractures beneath any of the head wounds and Freer formed the conclusion that the woman hadn't been dead when she fell. The surgeon felt that the woman had most likely been stunned by a blow to the front of her head and then thrown alive into the pit, where she subsequently died.

As yet, the identity of the woman was not known but, in the days prior to the discovery of her body, Michael Toll, an Irish peddler, had been making enquiries in the area about his missing common-law wife, Ann Cook.

According to Toll, he and Ann had been hawking their wares in the villages around Stourbridge on Monday 24 August when Ann had complained of a bad headache. The couple had rested for a while at a coal pit near Cradley then Ann had said she felt better so they had walked together to the turnpike road. There he had given Ann some shawls to sell and the couple had separated, having arranged to meet that evening at the Anchor public house at Stourbridge. He had last seen Ann as she set off to walk along the main Stourbridge road, while he took a different route to the town.

Toll had arrived at the Anchor at about half-past eight on the evening of 24 August and had immediately asked if his wife was there. When he was told that she hadn't been to the pub that day, he waited for a little while then announced his intention of going to look for her, saying that she might have gone to visit her father.

Pound Bridge, Cradley, 1944. (Author's collection)

Ann's father, Joseph, lived at Wolverley, about 5 miles outside Stourbridge. Toll arrived there at about four o'clock on the following morning and was told that Ann hadn't been there. So later that day he and Ann's sister, Jane, set off to look for her.

During the course of the day they asked at several places but nobody had seen any sign of Ann Cook. However, Jane and Michael were seen walking arm-in-arm near Stourbridge and Mrs Dorothy Harper, who knew Toll, jokingly threatened to tell his wife. Toll merely smiled, but when Mrs Harper asked where Ann was, he told her that he had left her in Stourbridge. It was race day and Mrs Harper then asked Toll if he and Ann would be going to the racecourse later on, to which Toll replied that they would.

Mrs Harper saw Toll again the following day, when he walked into the pub that she and her husband ran in Kidderminster. She served him with a glass of beer, then, noticing that he was looking round the pub, asked him what the matter was. Toll replied that he had left his wife in Stourbridge and had expected her to reach the pub before him.

When Toll heard that a body had been found, he went straight to the Swan Inn to see if it was Ann. Shown the woman's body, he immediately became distraught, kissing her forehead and crying, 'Oh, my dear Ann. Why didst thou leave me?' If she had stayed with him, he explained to onlookers, then she '... would not have been served this way.'

Toll was present at the inquest held by coroner Mr Hallen into Ann's death. He stated that he and Ann had never before had any 'ill words' and that he had left her at the turnpike road, planning to meet her later that evening at the Anchor. Yet for all his tears and apparent distress, there seemed to be something not quite right about Michael Toll's story. In trying to find the identity of the dead woman, the police had been asking questions in the area, to which they had received some very telling answers.

A woman had been seen sitting at the side of the pit on the evening of 24 August with a man whose description matched that of Michael Toll. Toll had also been seen alone by the pit some time later. When it became known that the police were making enquiries into Toll's whereabouts in the days after the body was found, Sarah Bucknell of the Union Inn, Kidderminster contacted them about Toll's stick, which he had left with her for safekeeping.

The stick was a peddler's wand, a stout oak stick with an iron ferrule and brass nails hammered into it marking the measurement of feet and inches. Sarah had placed the stick on a shelf behind the bar but, on hearing that Ann Cook was dead, she had taken it down to examine it more closely and seen what she believed was a bloodstain on one end of it. She had passed the stick to the local police officer, Constable John Yardley.

Two independent witnesses had since come forward to tell the police that they had seen and heard Michael Toll and Ann Cook arguing on the evening of 24 August and, when the investigating officers gave their evidence at the inquest, it prompted a verdict from the coroner's jury of wilful murder against Michael Toll.

Toll stood trial for the murder of Ann Cook before Mr Justice Littledale at the Worcester Assizes in March 1830. The prosecution, led by Mr Whateley, maintained that Toll had struck her over the head with his peddler's wand and then thrown her into the coal pit to die. For the next few days, he had kept up the pretence of searching for her in order to deflect suspicion from himself when her body was eventually found.

The prosecution called a number of witnesses, including the two people who had seen Toll and Cook quarrelling on the night of 24 August. Absalom Horner had seen the couple together in Cradley and when Toll had called at a house to show his wares Ann Cook had waited for him outside, looking frightened and uneasy. When Toll had left the house, he had marched off down the street seemingly indifferent to Ann Cook, leaving her to follow meekly behind him at a distance.

Sarah Westwood had seen the couple a short while later, Ann still walking dejectedly behind Michael. The two had been exchanging cross words and Sarah had heard Ann say, 'Lord, do you think I am a fool and don't know where I am going?' to which Toll retorted, 'If I have much more of your bother, I'll lay you down with this stick.' At this, Ann had burst into tears.

Joseph Billingham identified Michael Toll as the man that he had seen sitting by the pit with a woman and, having been taken to view the body of Ann Cook at the inquest, Billingham was able to positively state that Cook was the woman that he had been sitting with.

South Road, Stourbridge. (Author's collection)

Toll, who pleaded 'Not Guilty', stuck to his original statement to the police. He freely admitted that he and Ann had rested by the pit but continued to insist that he had last seen her as she set off to sell shawls on the main road to Stourbridge. Having called several character witnesses, all of whom spoke of Toll's good nature and humanity and stated that he and Ann seemed to be happy together, the defence rested by pointing out to the jury that Toll had initially gone to view Ann's body of his own free will and had made no attempt to abscond.

In summing up the case, the judge pointed out that most of the evidence against Michael Toll was circumstantial. However, he reminded the jury that Toll had given several different accounts of Ann's whereabouts following her alleged disappearance on 24 August. The jury deliberated only briefly before returning with a verdict of 'Guilty', at which Mr Justice Littledale passed the death sentence on Michael Toll, ordering that afterwards his body should be given for dissection. Accordingly, Toll was executed at Worcester on 12 March 1830.

4

'DON'T CRY, MY CHILD, AND I WILL GET YOU SOME FLOWERS'

Old Swinford, 1830

When the time came for the workers in the limestone pits at Old Swinford to have their breakfast, someone above ground would bang on the scaffolding at the surface. On 19 May 1830, miner Noah Stephens heard the noise that heralded his meal break and rushed eagerly to the bottom of the shaft. He was disappointed to see a bundle lying in the water there. Thinking that it was his breakfast, which had somehow accidentally fallen down the shaft, he found a stick and used it to pull the bundle towards him. However, as he picked the bundle up, he quickly realised that it was not his meal but the dead body of a child.

Startled, Stephens let out a yelp and dropped the body back into the water. He called his colleagues over to the bottom of the shaft and when he told them what he had found one of them waded into the water and rescued the bundle, which was taken to the surface. Once in daylight, they could see that it was the body of a little girl.

A surgeon was called, even though it was painfully obvious that the child was dead. Mr Freer from Stourbridge examined the little girl and found that she had a massive laceration on her scalp, beneath which her skull was fractured. The shaft down to the bottom of the limestone pit was 240ft deep and irregular, with numerous sizeable pieces of limestone sticking out of the sides. The surgeon felt that her injuries were consistent with either falling or being thrown down the shaft and that they were sufficiently serious to cause instantaneous death.

The police immediately knew the child's identity since a local girl had been reported missing just three days earlier. Five-year-old Sally Chance of Lye Waste had gone to visit a friend with her mother, Mary, and her mother's husband-to-be, Charles Wall.

The three had been at the home of Samuel Knowles from four o'clock in the afternoon until nine o'clock at night on Sunday 16 May. Sally had been running in and out of the house playing and, at about a quarter past eight, she asked her mother for some money to buy apples. Mary handed over a halfpenny and Sally went out, coming back a few minutes later with a bag of apples, which she gave to her mother. She then asked if she might go out to play again, to which her mother said yes.

Charles Wall left the house alone shortly afterwards. When Mary was ready to leave, she went looking for her daughter but couldn't find her. After half an hour of searching, she met up with Charles and asked him if he had seen Sally.

'Not since she brought you the apples,' replied Charles.

Charles Wall and Mary Chance searched high and low for Sally until about one o'clock in the morning, when Charles announced that he was going home to bed. Mary reluctantly went with him, spending a sleepless night, and the couple began the search for Sally again early the next morning.

In great distress, Mary walked from house to house, asking people if they had seen the child. One man, William 'Squirrel' Newey, told her, 'Mary, the last time I saw your child, she was with Charles Wall.' He went on to say that he had seen Wall with Sally close to the Anvil public house at a quarter to nine the previous night. Mary turned to Charles and asked him if this were true, but he denied it and walked away. Later that day, he paid a visit to William Newey alone and asked him, 'Well, Squirrel, did you see me with the child?'

Newey confirmed that he had. 'You're a damned liar!' Charles said to him and walked off before Newey had a chance to respond. He saw Charles again later the same day, in the company of a man named Josiah Hunt and, once again, Wall asked him the same question, again telling Newey that he was lying when he received the same reply.

Throughout the course of the day, several people came forward to say that they had seen Wall with the little girl on the Sunday evening. Thomas Kendrick had also seen him near the Anvil at about ten to nine. Sally had been walking a few yards behind Wall and he had called her to catch up. She ran towards him and Kendrick watched them climb over a stile heading towards the limestone pit and walk on together out of his sight.

William Baker had seen Charles and Sally close to the lime pit where she was last seen at around nine o'clock. By this time, Wall was carrying the child in his arms and she was crying bitterly, saying that she wanted to go home for her supper. Baker had taken particular notice of the couple on account of Sally's hysterical crying. Wall had comforted her, saying, 'Don't cry, my child, and I will get you some flowers.' Baker bade him 'Good night' but Wall did not answer.

An inquest into Sally Chance's death had already been held, at which William Baker had picked Charles Wall out of a line-up of thirteen or fourteen people as the man he had seen with the sobbing child. Consequently, the coroner's jury returned a verdict of 'wilful murder' against Wall and he was immediately arrested and committed for trial at the next Worcester Assizes.

The proceedings opened on 28 July 1830 before Mr Justice Park. Mr Whateley prosecuted, while Mr Carrington defended. Charles Wall, who was twenty-two years old and described as a 'mild-looking man', pleaded 'Not Guilty' to the charge against him.

The prosecution first called miners Noah Stephens and W. Mudford, who confirmed the circumstances of the discovery of Sally's body. The location of the pit was illustrated on a map of the parish presented to the court by John Davis. Then came a procession of witnesses who had all seen Sally with Charles Wall on the evening of 16 May. These included Maria Pearson, who had seen Sally playing on the side of the road with two other children. She saw Wall come out of Samuel Knowles's house and approach Sally, saying, 'Sally, your mother is gone home.'

'Is she?' asked Sally, and then walked off towards her home, with Wall following her.

William Newey and William Baker testified, as did John Round who had seen Wall returning from the direction of the limestone pit at just after nine o'clock. He was then alone.

Anne Southall was then called to the witness box. She was the wife of the clerk to the owner of the lime pits and she told the court that on the morning of 16 May, Wall had come to her house and asked questions about the pit, wanting to know if the road to it was 'stopped' and which of the pits was 'knocked off'. Mrs Southall told the court that it was well known in the area that the pit in which Sally had been found was a working pit and had been so for about two years. Noah Stephens was then recalled to confirm that the pit was 'in full work'.

Mary Chance gave her account of the night her daughter had disappeared. Mary had two illegitimate children, Sally and a younger child, who was then three years old. Neither of the children had been fathered by Charles Wall – Sally's father was a man named Wright Rubens.

Mary and Charles were engaged to be married and, although Charles did not contribute to the maintenance of either of her children, he had always treated them both kindly. Before the day of Sally's disappearance, Mary said that she had never known Charles to go off with her daughter alone.

The prosecution then attempted to call William Pritchard, a prisoner who had been incarcerated with Wall since his arrest and to whom Wall had allegedly spoken about the death of Sally Chance. However, before Pritchard could testify, the surgeon of the jail informed the court that Pritchard was almost completely deaf, prone to committing acts of violence and, in the surgeon's opinion, quite insane. Mr Justice Park determined that any contribution that Pritchard might make was not likely to be helpful to the case and refused to hear his testimony.

Next, John Yardley, the Old Swinford constable, testified to arresting Wall after the inquest and handing him over to the custody of William Westward. 'I shall surely be hung for this crime,' Wall told Westward.

Hagley Road, Old Swinford, 1917. (Author's collection)

Surgeon Mr Freer was the last prosecution witness, after which Mr Carrington began his defence.

For every witness that the prosecution had called, it seemed that the defence had a witness who had seen Sally Chance playing alone around the top of the unfenced mine shaft on the night of her disappearance.

Benjamin Robins was the first of these. Like Wall, he was a nailor by trade and he had known Wall for about ten years. According to Robins, Wall had always treated Sally Chance with kindness and appeared to be very fond of her. Robins told the court that he had seen several children playing near the mineshaft at around seven o'clock on 16 May, including Sally and one of his own children. He had taken his child home, leaving Sally at the pit. Under cross-examination, Robins said that he had seen Mary Chance at ten o'clock that night and was absolutely certain that he had told her that her daughter had been playing near the pit.

Josiah Hunt had known Sally from infancy and Charles Wall for fifteen years. Hunt too said that Charles had always treated Sally kindly, going as far as to say that Wall was kinder to Sally than he himself was to his own children. Stating that Wall was a very honest and humane man, Josiah Hunt said that he too had seen Sally Chance playing unsupervised near the shaft on the evening of 16 May.

Thomas Bolton had not seen Sally at all but he echoed Josiah Hunt's praise of Charles Wall.

Ten-year-old John Cartwright was next to testify. He was Wall's nephew and said that, on the night of Sally's disappearance, he had met his uncle at about nine o'clock at Hay Hill. His uncle had picked up John's younger brother, Henry, and carried him home. John and Henry's mother confirmed that her children had arrived home at between nine and ten o'clock that night.

After the defence had closed, Constable Yardley was recalled to the stand to answer a question about Benjamin Robins' testimony. Yardley stated that Robins had told him that he must keep Wall in custody, as he was the murderer of Mary Chance's child. According to Yardley, Robins had even offered to pay the costs. William Westward was then recalled and he stated that Robins had definitely told him that he had seen Sally playing near the mineshaft and had mentioned nothing about keeping Wall in custody.

It only remained for the judge to sum up the case for the jury. Mr Justice Park said that he was at a loss to know what motive the prisoner could have had for so diabolical a crime. He went on to say that motives could not be judged by earthly tribunal but were open only to that Eye that knew all secrets and from which nothing was hidden. If the jury believed that the prisoner threw the child down the pit, they must suppose it was from a malicious motive and find him guilty. If they believed that the child had fallen down accidentally, then they should acquit him. Several reliable witnesses had testified to seeing the defendant walking towards the pit with the child, then walking back alone, but, on the other hand, several equally reliable witnesses had testified to seeing Sally playing near the unguarded pit shaft before her disappearance and nobody had been called who could testify to anything but kindness and fondness shown towards the deceased child by the prisoner.

The jury were then dismissed to ponder this conundrum. However, before they retired, they asked for some clarification about the condition of the pit on the night of 16 May, wanting to know if it had been covered over, as, if it had, it would have been impossible for the child to fall in by accident.

Two witnesses were recalled, both of whom stated that it was normal practice for the pit to be left uncovered overnight.

The jury then retired for about fifteen minutes, returning to pronounce Charles Wall 'Guilty' of the wilful murder of Sally Chance but unanimously recommending mercy.

Mr Justice Park told the jury that in a case of murder he could receive no recommendations for mercy. There would be no mercy for Charles Wall in this world.

The judge then addressed Charles Wall, telling him that he believed that the jury had returned a proper verdict since, if Sally had fallen down the pit by accident, her playmates would have immediately raised the alarm. Mr Justice Park then passed the death sentence on Wall, ordering that afterwards his body should be given to the surgeons for dissection. Wall showed no emotion at the sentence, save for a slight quivering of his lip as he was escorted from the dock.

There was indeed to be no earthly mercy for Charles Wall, who was hanged at Worcester Prison on 30 July 1830.

5

'I PLANNED THE MURDER FOR DAYS AND EVEN DREAMED ABOUT IT'

Areley Kings, 1836

Seventy-year-old Joseph Hawkins had never married. After spending most of his life as a navigator at sea, he retired to the village of Areley Kings, where he opened a small grocer's shop. A pleasant, well-liked man, Joseph suffered from a lung disease that led him to cough and wheeze constantly and was so severe that he found lying down uncomfortable and so chose to spend his nights sleeping upright in his armchair.

Hawkins normally visited the market at Stourport every Wednesday and Saturday to buy stock for his shop and Wednesday 7 September 1836 was no exception. Early the following morning, he served a neighbour, William Randall, with some tobacco and, at seven o'clock, the local woman who did his housework called to collect his dirty clothes for washing. Elizabeth Giles, whose garden adjoined his, saw him pottering about outside later that morning. The next time he was seen was by William Randall at five o'clock in the evening. About four hours later, Randall heard what sounded like a gunshot coming from the direction of Hawkins' shop.

On Friday 9 September, Elizabeth Giles went round to the shop in the morning to buy some coffee and was surprised to find the door locked. She knew that Joseph Hawkins always left the key in the shop door while he was at home but, on that morning, there was no sign of the key, so Elizabeth assumed that he had gone out and

High Street, Stourport, in the 1920s. (Author's collection)

taken it with him. She left the shop, returning at about four o'clock in the afternoon fully expecting Mr Hawkins to be there to serve her.

The door was still locked and Elizabeth grew concerned for her neighbour's safety. She peered through the windows and noticed that some of the cupboard doors inside the shop were open, something that was most unusual since Hawkins was normally a very neat and orderly man. She went round to the backyard and tried to look through the window of an old brew house there, but a wheelbarrow that was propped up against the window inside the building blocked her view.

When Hawkins still hadn't returned by nine o'clock that evening, Elizabeth knew that there was something very wrong because the old man would always ask her to feed his pigs if he expected to be away from the shop for any length of time. She began to canvas the neighbours, asking if anyone had seen him and it quickly became apparent that he hadn't been seen at all that day.

Finally, local miller George Harris decided to investigate. Having tried all the doors and windows and found them locked, he procured a ladder and climbed up to the window of one of the rooms above the shop. While Elizabeth Giles, her husband and son and another near neighbour, William Lightband, waited anxiously below, Harris climbed up the ladder and shone a lantern through the window. There was no sign of Joseph Hawkins, although Harris did see two pairs of shoes inside the house.

Hawkins had only two pairs of shoes to his name, a stout outdoor pair and a lighter pair that he normally wore indoors. Thus it seemed that wherever Joseph Hawkins had gone, he had gone there without shoes on his feet.

The neighbours were unable to decide what to do for the best. Reluctant to break into the shop, they decided to wait until the following morning before doing anything, and, when there was still no sign of the shopkeeper, they called the police.

Two officers, Constable Hatton and Constable Purser, arrived in response to their report and, having borrowed a ladder, Hatton climbed to the bedroom and managed to prise open the window and gain entry. At first glance, there seemed to be nothing out of the ordinary, but when Hatton went downstairs, he found the shop in a state of disarray.

Cupboards stood open and their contents had been pulled out and scattered all around the shop. It looked as though Mr Hawkins had been attacked while he was weighing out sugar, since there was sugar everywhere and the scoop used to transfer it from its container to the scales was on the floor. Worryingly, large spots of blood mingled with the spilled sugar and there was yet more blood on the broad plank that served as the shop counter.

The policeman searched every room in the house, finding no trace of the missing man. He then went into the backyard and forced his way into the brew house where he finally found Joseph Hawkins lying face down on the floor, badly beaten and also apparently shot.

A doctor was sent for immediately, but there was nothing that he could do, since Hawkins had obviously been dead for some time. He had been bludgeoned so savagely about his head that his skull was smashed like an eggshell. One eye was almost beaten in and his stomach had been slashed, leaving his intestines hanging out. In addition, his clothes were peppered with small holes from gun pellets. He had numerous scratches on his hands and the front of his trousers was dirty, suggesting that he had been dragged from the shop to his present position.

There was evidence of violence throughout the brew house. A bloodstained coal hammer lay on the floor and a heavy stool leg was propped up in the corner of the room, covered with clotted blood and human hair. Whoever had attacked Mr Hawkins had then deliberately placed the wheelbarrow up against the window to prevent anybody from seeing the carnage from outside.

An inquest into the death of Joseph Hawkins was opened later that afternoon by coroner Mr Hallen and later adjourned to allow the police more time to conduct their enquiries. A post-mortem examination on Mr Hawkins revealed the true extent of his injuries. It seemed that he had initially been shot in the stomach, although by a miracle, the gunshot itself had caused very little internal damage. The cause of his death was deemed to be the horrendous beating he had received after being shot, which had resulted in numerous skull fractures, a broken breastbone and a ruptured liver.

As one of Mr Hawkins's closest neighbours, one of the first people to be interviewed was William Lightband who, conveniently for the police, was attending the inquest and was initially spoken to in the bar of the Stourport Inn, where the inquest was held. Lightband worked as a carpenter but had been off work due to an injured foot. He told the police that, on the day of Joseph Hawkins's murder, he had returned to work for the first time after a three-day absence. However, Lightband's alibi was soon shaken when others at the inquest told the police that they had seen him near his home at around eleven o'clock on the morning on which Hawkins was killed.

Inspector William Merrifield asked Lightband for an explanation and found him unable to provide one. He was detained, along with his wife, and searched. He was carrying a purse that, along with a pawn ticket, contained an unexpectedly large sum of money – two sovereigns, a half sovereign, seven shillings and sixpence. When the Inspector asked him how he had come by such a considerable sum, Lightband answered tersely, 'I worked for it.' The Inspector was not convinced, even less so when he found that Lightband had a decent silver watch in his pocket.

Merrifield went with Constable Hatton to Lightband's home, arriving at eleven o'clock and began a search of the premises, which lasted until midnight and then resumed early the following morning. Like Hawkins' home, Lightband had a brew house in the backyard, which he used as a workshop. There the police found a roll of tobacco, and a gun, which had been broken into several parts. Even so, the gun smelled as though it had been recently fired. They also found a covered basket containing a bag of raisins and a similar bag of currants.

Merrifield returned to ask Lightband how these items came to be in his possession. 'If they are in my house, I know nothing about them,' was his reply. 'They must have been put there by some person.' However, shortly afterwards Lightband indicated that he wished to speak to the Inspector. 'I want to unburden my mind,' he told him and proceeded to make a full confession to the murder of Joseph Hawkins.

'I planned the murder for days and even dreamed about it,' he said and then went on to dictate a full statement to Constable Dukens, who wrote it down. Lightband told how, having injured his foot at work by dropping a large log onto it, he had made a special trip to Stourport on the Monday before the murder, visiting three different shops to buy powder, percussion caps and shot for his gun. He had hidden the gun in his brew house, covering it with a piece of cloth, but his toddler son had repeatedly pulled the cloth away, for which he had eventually given the boy a spanking.

On the Tuesday, his wife had been out hop picking all day and Lightband said that two or three times during the course of that day he had seen Joseph Hawkins working in his garden and gone to give him a hand. The last time had been about six o'clock in the evening, when he had taken his gun with him to Hawkins's shop and asked the old man for half a pound of cheese. As Hawkins cut it, Lightband drew his gun and aimed at him, but the gun had misfired.

Hawkins obviously thought that Lightband was playing a joke on him, as he had laughed and told him to put the gun away. Lightband fixed his gun on the Wednesday and, when his wife asked him if he was going back to work the following day, he told her that he was. However, although he left for work as normal, he had hidden until his wife had gone off hop picking, before doubling back to his home.

Lightband waited until that evening before going into the shop again and asking Hawkins for half a pound of sugar. As Hawkins weighed out the sugar, he had shot him once and then hit him over the head with the gun, breaking the stock in the process. He then dragged Hawkins into the brew house, but, because the old man was making a noise, he had hit him repeatedly about his chest and belly with the coal hammer. Hawkins continued to groan, so Lightband belaboured him with the stool leg until he was finally quiet.

Lightband went into the shop and rifled the till, taking about 20s 10d. He then locked up the shop and left, taking the key with him. On the following day, he went back into the shop to search upstairs, finding five sovereigns and a £5 note. He had checked on Joseph Hawkins and found him dead so, having stolen tobacco and groceries from the shop, he locked the door again and took the key to Stourport, where he threw it into the River Severn. He had then dismantled his gun and burnt the stock to make it appear as though it could not be used.

'This is the truth, so help me God,' he ended. 'No person on earth knew anything about it and nor have I had any accomplice. My wife is utterly ignorant of everything concerning it.' Lightband, who was illiterate, then signed his confession with a cross.

The entire confession was obtained and an arrest was made before the resumption of the inquest and when Inspector Merrifield relayed his progress in the investigations into the murder to the coroner, the jury had no hesitation in returning a verdict of wilful murder against William Lightband and committing him for trial at the next assizes. He was taken to Worcester Gaol to await the start of legal proceedings against him. Before he left, he asked if he might see his wife, but his request was refused. The refusal was met with a flood of tears and, within moments, Lightband collapsed. It was the only emotion that he had shown since his arrest.

Twenty-eight-year-old Lightband was said by his wife to be a tender and loving husband. At the time of the murder, she was expecting their second child and she subsequently gave birth while her husband was incarcerated. He originally came from Dudley and had been apprenticed to a wheelwright and sawyer in Bromsgrove. However, he had run away before completing his apprenticeship and had since made his living as a carpenter, earning up to 30s a week. This was a good wage at the time, but Lightband had chosen to spend his time drinking in the local pubs rather than working. With a young child and another on the way, robbing Joseph Hawkins had seemed like an easier way than carpentry to obtain money.

His trial took place at Worcester, opening on 6 March 1837, and Lightband pleaded 'Not Guilty' to the murder of Joseph Hawkins. However, the evidence against him, coupled with his confession, was compelling. It had emerged that, immediately after the murder, Lightband, who was notorious in the area for running up debts, which he then didn't pay, had been spending money very freely. He had paid off arrears in his rent, amounting to nearly £3, and bought the silver watch found on him at the time of his arrest for £2. He had even purchased a new hat and ordered a set of monogrammed handkerchiefs from a draper in Stourport.

The jury had no hesitation in finding him 'Guilty of wilful murder'. Lightband sobbed piteously throughout his trial, particularly when he heard the judge pronounce sentence of death upon him.

The church at Areley Kings where Joseph Hawkins is buried in an unmarked grave. (Author's collection)

While incarcerated, Lightband had learned to read for the first time in his life and in the last few days remaining to him, he read his Bible avidly. He showed extreme remorse for his crime, acknowledging that the sentence he had been given was just and fair.

Two days before his scheduled execution, Lightband was visited by his wife and mother. It was a traumatic meeting and, when the time came for his wife to go, Lightband clung desperately to her, heartbroken at the thought of her leaving him for the very last time.

On the eve of his execution, a heavy snow fell throughout the area, in spite of which a crowd numbering more than 8,000 people arrived at Worcester Prison on the morning of 23 March 1837 to witness his hanging. Lightband marched resolutely to the scaffold but, as the executioner drew the hood over his face, his courage deserted him and, according to *The Times*, '...it seemed that every muscle in his frame was vibrating with the mental agony that devoured him within.' He repeated the words 'Lord, have mercy upon me' again and again until the trap door fell, killing him instantly. After hanging for the customary period, his body was cut down, his hair shaved and plaster casts were made of his head before his body was finally buried within the confines of the prison walls.

Note: Various contemporary accounts of the murder give different ages for William Lightband, who is alternatively described as aged twenty-eight, aged thirty and 'not above thirty-five years of age'.

6

'WHAT WAS I TO DO, KICKED AND ABUSED AS I WAS?'

Rous Lench, 1842

In the 1840s, the farmers in and around the village of Rous Lench were greatly troubled by foxes and, whenever anybody managed to trap a live fox, it was customary for the animal to be taken on a tour of the farms where the farmers would usually reward its captors with money or goods for their efforts. This was the case on 11 December 1842, when a group of young men carried a fox in a sack around the local farms.

The eight men – John Court, William and Charles Tandy, Edwin Archer, George Green, John Clarke and John and George Bullock – were in high spirits as they paraded the animal from farm to farm. In the afternoon, they called at the Bell Inn, Rous Lench, where they stayed until four o'clock when, apparently still perfectly sober, they set off again towards Radford. They had gone only a few hundred yards when George Green and Edwin Archer began a play fight, during the course of which both men fell to the ground.

John Court walked past them, telling them, 'Come along and let us have no nonsense.' He was ahead of the two men by about 20–30 yards when he heard George Green cry out, 'I am stabbed.'

Court turned to see Green bent over, clutching his stomach. Green staggered a few steps and then fell to his hands and knees, saved only from plunging headfirst into the roadside ditch by the quick reactions of John Clarke, who grabbed him around the waist as he pitched forward. Edwin Archer stood as if frozen to the spot, a knife in his hands.

27

Court immediately ran to the nearest cottage where he roused Mrs Sarah Pardoe, who rushed to see if she could help. By the time she reached the scene of the fight, George Green was still on all fours in the middle of the lane, prevented only from falling over by John Clarke, who was still supporting him by the waist. When Clarke released his hold, Green immediately slumped to the ground. Edwin Archer was sitting in the road, crying bitterly. Mrs Pardoe asked Edwin how he could do such a thing, to which Archer answered tearfully, 'What was I to do, kicked and abused as I was?'

John Griffin, a tailor from Inkberrow, happened to walk past and, having sent one of the men for the Inkberrow doctor, continued to the police house at Rous Lench. Constable Whadcoat was not at home but returned within a few minutes and immediately went to find the men, who by now had placed George Green on a gate and carried him to the Bell Inn. Although Dr Cooper was only minutes later in arriving, he was sadly too late to save Green.

Cooper conducted a post-mortem examination later that day and found that Green had been stabbed four times with a weapon similar to an American bowie knife. He had a deep wound just above his navel, which had penetrated his body almost through to his spine. A second stab had entered his left armpit, glancing off his ribs, and there was a further wound above his left hip. The fatal injury was to his left breast, where the knife had entered his body just below his nipple and penetrated his heart.

Constable Whadcoat notified his superior officer at Pershore of the situation at Rous Lench and Superintendent William Harris promptly came to help. Between

Rous Lench. (© N. Sly, 2008)

them, the two officers arrested all of Green's companions, who all seemed completely stunned by what had just happened to their friend. Archer in particular was distraught. All of the men were of previous good character, although most, if not all of them, indulged in a little poaching from time to time.

None of the men had seen the stab wounds being inflicted on George Green and none had seen Archer with a knife in his possession before the stabbing occurred. When Archer was searched on his arrest, no knife was found, so the police began a fingertip search of the area, draining ditches, clearing scrub and cutting back hedges in their quest to find the murder weapon. On the day after the murder, a knife was found at the bottom of a ditch.

It was a large clasp knife with a straight, 4in long blade and a horn handle. Having been immersed in water, it bore no trace of blood but, according to Dr Cooper, was entirely consistent with the weapon that had produced Green's wounds.

An inquest was opened before the coroner, Mr C. Best, at the Bell Inn, at which the coroner struggled to find anyone who knew anything whatsoever about the killing of George Green. None of his companions knew of any animosity between Green and Archer, nobody had heard any threats made between them and nobody had seen the actual stabbing.

Constable Joseph Bradford of Pershore was the only man who seemed able to throw any light on the killing. Left alone with Archer at Pershore police station, Bradford told the inquest that Archer had told him that he had never stabbed George Green nor had he intended to. He had been using the knife to scrape mud off his trousers and Green had run at him, at which the knife had accidentally gone into Green's body. (This explanation obviously fails to account for the fact that Green was stabbed four times!)

The coroner's jury of twenty-one men returned a verdict of wilful murder against Edwin Archer, who was committed on a Coroner's Warrant to stand trial at the next county assizes. As there was no evidence of culpability against the other men, they were all discharged.

However, before Archer's case came to court, it was placed before the Grand Jury, whose job it was to determine whether or not there was actually a case to answer. To everyone's surprise, the Grand Jury determined that there wasn't. Thus, when Edwin Archer made his appearance at the Worcester Assizes on 9 March 1843, before Mr Justice Wightman, it was to answer to a charge of manslaughter, to which he pleaded 'Guilty' and was sentenced to transportation for fifteen years.

7

'HAVE YOU SEEN MY LITTLE WHORE?'

Drakes Broughton, 1848

Mary Ann Staight was an orphan who lived with her aunt, Mrs Elizabeth Richards, at Drakes Broughton, near Pershore and, although she was illegitimate, fifteen-year-old Mary Ann's own character was described as 'without blemish'.

On 5 December 1848, at about four o'clock in the afternoon, Mary Ann's aunt asked her to run an errand to the village shop. Mary Ann put on her silk bonnet, picked up a basket and took 6d from her aunt to pay for the groceries that she needed. Elizabeth accompanied her niece outside and watched for a few moments as the girl walked off towards the shop. Little did Elizabeth know that this would be the last time she would ever see the girl alive.

Almost as soon as she left the house, Mary Ann passed a man who had been standing at the corner of her aunt's garden. He was forty-nine-year-old labourer, Robert Pulley and, in the past, there had been bad blood between him and Mary Ann, whom he had accused of meddling in his affairs and of being a whore. However, on this occasion, the two passed without speaking.

Mary Ann called in to visit Ann Turvey on her way to the shop, staying for about half an hour. She then continued to Mrs Tyler's shop, which was about a mile from her aunt's house. Having purchased the tea, sugar and a paper packet of pins that her aunt had asked for, Mary Ann had a brief chat with the shopkeeper then set off to walk home again at around five o'clock.

It was now dark and, when Mary Ann didn't arrive home as expected, her worried aunt immediately retraced her steps to the village shop. Learning that Mary Ann had left the shop some time earlier, she slowly walked the girl's route home, all the while calling her niece's name. For that night and for most of the following day, people combed the village and the surrounding lanes searching for the missing girl, but she seemed to have disappeared without a trace.

It was not until the afternoon of 6 December that Ann Turvey's eight-year-old son, Frederick, who was employed as a bird-scarer, noticed something unusual at the side of the road from Pershore to Worcester. When he went for a closer look, he could see a bare arm sticking out of a ditch. Frederick ran straight home to fetch his mother who immediately went to check her son's story.

Mary Ann Staight had been found. Her basket was found in the same ditch about 200 yards from her body. Apart from a missing packet of pins, her groceries were still intact.

The police were called and Mary Ann's body was removed from the ditch. A post-mortem examination was performed by Mr John Claridge, a surgeon from Pershore, who found that Mary Ann had a swelling the size of a walnut on her forehead, just above her right eye, along with a 3½in wound on the top of her head. There were corresponding depressed fractures beneath both wounds and pieces of the girl's skull had been driven into her brain at the sites of both injuries, the resulting damage to her brain being cited by the surgeon as the cause of her death.

As was the custom before the relatively modern concept of preserving the crime scene, over the next few days, curious villagers flocked to the site where Mary Ann's body had been discovered. Among them was thirteen-year-old Frederick Taylor, who went to look at the site with his father four days after the discovery of the body. Roughly 20 yards from where the body had been found, the Taylors noticed a stout stick, lying in a ditch on the opposite side of the lane. When they retrieved the stick, they saw that there were two or three long, light brown hairs sticking to one end.

Pershore, 1950s. (Author's collection)

Drakes Broughton. (© N. Sly, 2008)

The stick was about a 1ft long and 3in in diameter, with a knob at one end and weighed 1¼lbs.

The stick was handed to the police, who immediately passed it to Mr Claridge. When he examined it, the surgeon found a lump in the wood that corresponded exactly with the depressed fracture in Mary Ann's skull and he also noted that the hairs stuck to the end of the stick matched her hair perfectly.

Meanwhile, the police had been making enquiries in the village and had come to the conclusion that Robert Pulley was involved in Mary Ann's murder. Pulley was known to dislike the young girl intensely and a number of people told the police that they had seen him following her as she walked either to or from the shop on the day of her death. Yet more people had seen him hanging around close to where her body was eventually discovered.

James Savage, a general labourer, told the police that he had met Pulley at between four and five o'clock on the evening of the murder and that, while they were talking, Mary Ann had walked past them. Pulley had shouted after her, 'You be going off again tonight, be you? You'll have it before you come back.' Mary Ann had walked past without responding and, when she had gone, Pulley had told Savage that she was a 'damned whore' who had been seen in the lane with her skirts up around her waist and that he would like to 'spread her brains in the road'.

William Simpson, the local butcher, had also seen Pulley at around the same time. Pulley had walked past him as he worked in a field at the side of the lane and shouted to Simpson, 'Have you seen my little whore?' Simpson told Pulley that Mary

Ann had passed by only a few minutes earlier. He noticed that Pulley was carrying a hatchet in his hand, which Pulley told him he would like to put through Mary Ann's head. 'If I light on her tonight, I'll give her a snowler,' he told Mr Simpson. Neither Simpson nor Savage took Pulley's threats seriously, since Pulley was known in the village for his 'wicked talk'.

Since Pulley was nowhere to be found in the village, the police set out to track him down. They discovered that he had called at the Coach and Horses public house in Pershore at about seven o'clock in the morning on 6 December. Ann Cook, a servant at the inn, recalled Pulley asking for a pint of cider, which he drank and then asked for a second. He had paid for his drinks with half a crown and, on being given his change, had dropped some of it on the floor. Ann had picked up a candle, intending to give him some light by which to find the dropped money, but Pulley had said that he could find the money without her help. Nevertheless, she held the candle for him and, as he reached forward to pick up the coins from the floor, she had noticed some blood on the cuff of his shirt. As soon as Pulley had seen Ann looking at his shirt, he had hurriedly pushed his sleeve up his arm, out of her sight. Ann told the police that Pulley had spent about two hours at the pub and that he had seemed distracted and nervous, particularly when other customers came in and began talking about the startling discovery of a body at Drakes Broughton.

Robert Pulley was eventually located on Thursday 7 December, hiding beneath some loose straw in a barn in the neighbouring parish of Pinvin. Constable William Crowther and Superintendent W. Harris of the Worcestershire Constabulary apprehended him and escorted him back to the police station at Pershore, where he was searched. He was found to have 1s 4½d in coins in his pockets and was wearing two smock frocks and a waistcoat over two shirts. The outer smock had what appeared to be bloodstains on the cuffs and other small spots of blood were found on the rest of his clothes. Charged with the wilful murder of Mary Ann Staight, Robert Pulley immediately denied having anything to do with the girl's death.

At the inquest, held before the coroner, Charles Best, the jury returned a verdict of wilful murder against forty-nine-year-old Pulley and he was committed for trial at the next Worcester Assizes, which opened before Mr Justice Coltman on 8 March 1849. Mr Whitmore and Mr Huddleston prosecuted the case, while Mr W.H. Cooke appeared for the defence. The case aroused a great deal of interest in the area and people stampeded to try and get a place as a spectator.

Mr Whitmore opened the case for the prosecution by describing Mary Ann's last journey and telling the jury that Robert Pulley had 'not scrupled day after day to express in most violent terms not only his aversion to the girl but even his intention to do her injury.' Quite why Pulley had such an intense dislike of the girl was not clear and, Whitmore said, it was not his place to speculate. He then went on to do exactly that, suggesting that perhaps Pulley had failed to win her affections or obtain her favours.

Whitmore then went on to call his witnesses for the prosecution, who included Elizabeth Richards, the dead girl's aunt, shopkeeper Hannah Tyler and several of the villagers of Drakes Broughton who had seen or spoken to either Mary Ann or Pulley on the night of the murder.

In the course of their enquiries into the case, the police had traced the owner of the stick used as the murder weapon. Thomas Panter told the court that he had owned the stick for about eight years and that he used it as a mallet to drive stakes into the ground. He had last seen his stick on 16 November, when Pulley had been working for him, turning his garden in preparation for planting potatoes. On that day, Mary Ann Staight had spoken to Panter, asking him for permission to walk through his garden. After she had gone through, Pulley asked Panter if she had said anything about him and, when told that she hadn't, immediately launched into a verbal attack about her to Panter, telling him that Mary Ann was a 'crank young bitch' who would be better off dead. Her aunt would ruin her, said Pulley, and, if he had his way, he would 'give her a topper.'

Panter was cross-examined by the counsel for the defence about his ability to recall the exact date of this conversation. Panter told him that he could recall it perfectly, since it took place on the day of his wedding anniversary. He had searched high and low for his stick when he realised it was missing, even checking under the soil that Pulley had turned in case it had been buried.

Coroner Best was then called to tell the court that, at the inquest, he had asked Pulley about Panter's stick and Pulley had stated that he had thrown it into the pear trees that edged Panter's garden. Recalled, Panter admitted that he had not thought to search among the branches of the trees for his stick.

John Claridge imparted the results of his post-mortem examination of the victim, to which he added a few extra details about her injuries. He told the court that it was his opinion that the girl had been pole-axed from behind by a blow from Panter's stick, struck by someone who was much taller than she. The wounds would have been bloody, but Mary Ann's bonnet would have contained the majority of the blood, hence he would not have expected her attacker to have much blood on him. Having examined the bonnet, he had been unable to find much blood on it, since it was wet through, but he believed that the stains on Robert Pulley's smock were consistent with the amount of blood that would have splashed from Mary Ann's wounds.

At the request of Mr Cooke, Ann Turvey was recalled to the witness box. It had been her son who had found the body and she had immediately gone to check his story when he returned home and told her of his find. Mrs Turvey testified to seeing Mary Ann's bonnet, which she described as a silk bonnet with a pasteboard front. The back of the bonnet was almost completely torn away from the front and had contained a considerable quantity of blood.

Mr Cooke was then left to defend the prisoner. He began his defence by saying that he was not intending to deny that a murder had been committed, nor was he intending to deny that Mary Ann had died at the hands of his client. However, at the time of the murder, Robert Pulley had not been responsible for his actions.

Cooke pointed out the lack of motive for the murder, ridiculing the prosecution's opening statement in which it was intimated that Mary Ann Staight might, in the past, have rejected Pulley's advances. Pulley was a destitute man in his fiftieth year who had no home and customarily slept in barns, wherever he could lay his head. He was an uneducated casual worker, who was maintained mainly by the charity of others. What reason would he have to think of himself as an attractive proposition to a well-educated girl of fifteen? Neither was robbery the motive, since the only thing missing was a packet of pins. Cooke admitted that, although the pins were probably the most likely objects for a lunatic to have taken, they had not been found on Pulley when he was apprehended.

Only a lunatic, said Cooke, would have made so many public threats against someone and then gone on to murder that person. Only a lunatic would have followed his victim so openly. Only a lunatic would return to within a mile of the murder rather than fleeing. Since his arrest, Pulley had made several rambling statements, none of which had made much sense to anybody. He was regarded as a lunatic in the community, particularly since he had been ill with typhus fever some years previously. Here was a man who had done many strange things in the past – he constantly talked about murder, had burned all his clothes and had destroyed all his work tools on occasions – and yet witness after witness had said in court that they hadn't taken him seriously. The villagers of Drakes Broughton had long known that Pulley was a lunatic – unfortunately, they had made the mistake of believing that he wasn't a dangerous lunatic.

In his summary of the case, the judge told the jury that there were but two important matters to consider. The first was whether or not they were convinced that Mary Ann Staight had died at Pulley's hands. If the jury were so convinced, they should then decide if Pulley was responsible for his actions at the time of the murder. The judge pointed out that, although Pulley's actions did not seem like those of a sane man, not one of the villagers who had testified in court had intimated that he was regarded as a lunatic.

The jury needed only ten minutes to decide that they believed that Pulley was sane and, to the consternation of the majority of the spectators in court, returned a verdict of 'Guilty of Wilful Murder' against Robert Pulley.

The judge turned to Pulley and asked him, 'What motive could have operated in your mind to induce you to kill this innocent young person just starting out in life?' He then ordered that Pulley should be hanged by the neck until dead and his body buried within the confines of the prison walls. Pulley accepted the sentence with the same indifference he had exhibited throughout the proceedings. He was executed on 26 March 1849, without ever revealing the answer to the judge's question.

8

'HOW COULD YOU BE SUCH A CRUEL MOTHER?'

Near Stourbridge, 1852

On 4 June 1852, Mary Ann Robins – or Mary Ann Richards, as she was sometimes known – gave birth to a daughter, Lucy, at the Union Workhouse in Wolverhampton. Lucy was a fine, healthy baby, although on 18 June she suffered a brief bout of convulsions, from which she soon recovered.

On 19 June, Mary carefully washed and dressed her baby and left the workhouse, telling staff that she was intending to visit her mother. Four days later, the body of a female infant was discovered lying submerged in the standing water at the bottom of a 46ft-deep fire clay pit near Stourbridge.

A post-mortem examination was conducted on the baby, who was found to have numerous contusions on her tiny body, along with a severe head injury and massive brain damage, parts of her brain having been reduced almost to a pulp. The contused wounds did not appear to be at all discoloured, leading the doctor to believe that they had been inflicted after the child was dead, since he would normally have expected to see bruising had the child been injured while alive.

The police enquiries quickly led them to Mary Robins, who had arrived at her mother's house days earlier without her baby. When the police first interviewed her there on 23 June, she insisted, 'I have not had a child for two years.' She later amended her statement to say that she had recently given birth to a child, but it had died after being put into a warm bath and had subsequently been buried at Bilston, in the same grave as an old man, who had died from a fever.

High Street, Stourbridge, 1940s. (Author's collection)

At the time of Mary's first interview with the police, the body of the baby girl had still not been formally identified. However, Mary's conflicting statements were sufficient to arouse the suspicions of the investigating officers, who promptly paid a visit to the Wolverhampton workhouse. On 26 June, staff and nurses working there were taken to view the child's body at Stourbridge police station and were able to positively identify it as that of Lucy Richards. When Mary encountered the workhouse staff at the police station, she promptly fainted.

When Mary was asked to explain how her baby had ended up in the pit, she told various different versions of the events leading up to the child's death, the most consistent of which seemed to be that, while walking to her mother's home, she had sat down to suckle her daughter, who had begun to convulse and had subsequently died in a fit. Unsure of what to do with her daughter's dead body, Mary had disposed of it by tossing it into the pit. However, when Ann Manley, one of the workhouse nurses, asked her, 'How could you be such a cruel mother?' Mary replied, 'The devil tempted me and I threw it into the pit.'

Mary Robins was charged with the wilful murder of her daughter, Lucy, and appeared at the Worcester Assizes on 21 July 1852, before Mr Justice Cresswell. Mr Whitmore and Mr Best appeared for the prosecution, while Mr Huddleston defended the accused.

It was the contention of the defence that baby Lucy had died naturally from convulsions and that her mother had simply rid herself of her daughter's body by throwing it into the pit. However, the jury couldn't accept that version of events and, after retiring for a brief deliberation, returned a verdict of 'Guilty of Wilful Murder' against Mary Robins. They tempered their verdict with a recommendation

HIGH STREET, STOURBRIDGE.

Stourbridge, 1917. (Author's collection)

for mercy, on the grounds that they believed that Mary Robins was of weak intellect, albeit fully capable of responsible understanding. Promising to forward the jury's recommendation to the proper quarters, but telling them that he held out no hope that the sentence would not be carried out, Mr Justice Cresswell then sentenced Mary Robins to death.

As Mary waited in Worcester Prison for her execution, strenuous efforts were being made on her behalf by her defence counsel to secure a reprieve. Mr Huddleston appealed to Mr Justice Cresswell to intervene, but the judge declined to interfere with the course of justice. An application was made to the Secretary of State to appeal for a pardon for Mary Robins, on the grounds of her probable insanity and in view of the fact that Lucy could possibly have died from natural causes before her mother threw her into the pit.

Just days before her scheduled execution, the Secretary of State commuted Mary Robins' sentence to one of detention in a lunatic asylum. Interestingly, in 1861, the name Mary Ann Robins appears on the census records of Coton Hill Asylum in Staffordshire, however as a 'Watchwoman', rather than as a patient. Unfortunately, it is not possible to establish whether or not this is the same Mary Ann Robins who was detained pending Her Majesty's pleasure for the murder of her daughter, just nine years earlier.

9

'I HAVE HEARD THEM SAY REVENGE IS SWEET'

Dudley, 1855

By May 1855, seventeen-year-old Mary Ann Mason had been working as a servant at the Sailor's Return public house at Kate's Hill, Dudley, for about seven weeks. She was quiet and hard working, although her employers, William and Mary Hunt, did notice that whenever her brother visited her, she could be a little standoffish and would often practically ignore the young man.

This was the case on Friday 11 May. Joseph spent the evening in the pub, but Mary Ann barely acknowledged his presence and hardly spoke a word to him all night. Joseph sat at the bar drinking and talking to anyone who would listen about guns, shells and war. Mary Hunt caught snatches of his conversation as she occasionally walked past him and formed the conclusion that the young man didn't really know what he was talking about. Joseph, who was engaged as an apprentice whitesmith, eventually rolled home at two o'clock on the Saturday morning, completely intoxicated. His boss, Joseph Rann, let him in and left him on the sofa to sleep it off but, by the time Rann got up the next morning, there was no sign of his apprentice.

Joseph had gone back to the Sailor's Return and was served some ale at about ten minutes to seven on the morning of 12 May. He sat in the kitchen for some time, watching Mary Ann, who was busy mopping the floor and who, once again, had very little to say to him, acting as if she was displeased to see him. Mary Hunt was helping her servant clean the kitchen and briefly left the room to fetch something. When she got back, she saw to her horror that Joseph was holding a rifle and was in the process of raising it to point directly at his sister.

Dudley, 1926. (Author's collection)

Before Mary Hunt could shout a warning, there was a blinding flash and a deafeningly loud bang and Mary Ann Mason fell to the floor. Joseph immediately dropped the gun, which was picked up by another customer, William Robinson. William Hunt was in another part of the pub but came rushing into the kitchen at the sound of the gunshot. He bravely grabbed Joseph by his collar, shouting at him, 'You vagabond – you've shot your own sister!'

'I've done what I intended to do,' said Joseph calmly and quietly. 'Now I'm satisfied.'

The police were summoned and Constable Jukes arrested Joseph and took him into custody. He told the constable that his name was Joseph Meadows, not Joseph Mason, and that Mary Ann Mason wasn't his sister but was actually his girlfriend of ten months. 'She should have given me an answer,' Meadows said then continued, 'I've had my revenge. I have heard them say revenge is sweet.'

Searched at the police station, Meadows was found to be carrying a powder flask and a few caps for the rifle in his pockets. He told Jukes that the gun belonged to his employer and that, having shot Mary Ann he had dropped it, intending to go to her but had been prevented from doing so by William Hunt. 'I was determined if I could not have her, nobody else should,' Meadows said. Jukes charged him with shooting Mary Ann Mason but, within the hour, the charge was elevated to one of wilful murder.

Back at the pub, Mary Ann had lay bleeding heavily on the kitchen floor. Mr Johnson, a surgeon from Dudley, rushed to attend her and found that the single shot from the carbine rifle had hit her on the side of her head, penetrating some of the major blood vessels and causing a massive haemorrhage. She died within minutes of the surgeon's arrival and, when he conducted a post-mortem examination later that day, Johnson found that her ear lobe had been shot clean off, the shot then penetrating her jugular vein and carotid artery. Some of the shot had penetrated her ear, shattering the small bones within into fragments. Mary Ann had other fractured facial bones and her jaw had been damaged, as had the nerves that controlled the movement of her tongue, preventing her from speaking. According to Johnson, her death had resulted from loss of blood due to gunshot wounds.

The inquest into Mary Ann's death was opened later that same day and the coroner's jury returned a verdict of 'wilful murder' against Joseph Meadows, who was committed on the coroner's warrant to be tried at the next assizes.

His trial opened at Worcester before Chief Justice Baron Pollock on 18 July 1855. Mr Huddleston and Mr Cresswell appeared for the prosecution, while Mr Kettle took on the seemingly impossible charge of defending the accused.

The prosecution called Mary and William Hunt, William Robinson and William Ingram, another customer of the pub who had witnessed the shooting, Constable Jukes testified to arresting Meadows, while Joseph Rann told the court that his apprentice had been extremely intoxicated when he saw him just a few hours before the murder and, when he had seen him again at lunchtime on the day of the murder, he had still seemed far from sober.

Finally, Mr Johnson dealt with the medical evidence and it was left to the two opposing counsels to sum up the case for the jury.

Given that Joseph Meadows had been seen to shoot Mary Ann Mason by three witnesses and that he had immediately confessed to the murder, both to the witnesses

Dudley, 1940s. (Author's collection)

Dudley in the 1950s. (Author's collection)

and then to the police, both speeches were, not surprisingly, very short. Counsel for the prosecution merely summed up the witnesses' statements, then Mr Kettle, the counsel for the defence, warned the jury that they should not place too much reliance on statements made by the defendant while he was obviously under the influence of drink.

After the judge had summarised the case, the jury took less than five minutes to return with a verdict of 'Guilty of Wilful Murder' against Joseph Meadows. The judge commented that this was one of the clearest cases ever to have come before a criminal court and that Meadows had obviously premeditated the murder before committing it. He then sentenced Joseph Meadows to death.

Once in prison, Joseph wrote a long, rambling letter of confession to Mary Ann's parents. He and Mary Ann had, according to Meadows, been very much in love but had concealed their true relationship because she believed that her parents would not have approved. When Mary Ann got her job at the pub, he had become suspicious of her friendliness towards the other male customers and, after a long session of drinking, followed by a sleepless night throughout which he had lain awake, brooding over her imagined infidelity, he had been overwhelmed with jealousy and borrowed his employer's gun, determined to finally claim her as his own.

Twenty-three-year-old Joseph Meadows went to the gallows on 28 July 1855. As he met executioner William Calcraft on the scaffold, he begged him 'Do it quickly'. Calcraft duly obliged.

10

'HER AIN'T DEAD, IS HER?'

Oldbury, 1862

By 1862, William Ockold had been married to his wife, Sophia, for nearly fifty years. The couple's children had long since grown up and left home, leaving William and Sophia to live together in their small rented cottage at Halesowen Street in Oldbury, which was described in the contemporary newspapers as 'a wretched little hovel'. The Ockold's lived in poverty, although the main reason for their acute lack of money was that most of William's earnings as a tailor, plus the 2s 6d the couple received weekly from the parish, were spent on drink.

In early November 1862, Sophia fell ill. Over the previous four or five years, the Ockolds had become very close to a young woman named Maria Grazebrook, who worked as a servant at the nearby George and Dragon public house, so much so that, although they were not related to her in any way, Maria referred to them as grandmother and grandfather. Maria called on the couple on the afternoon of 7 November and found Sophia sitting on the floor, her head resting on a bench, groaning in apparent pain. Concerned, Maria asked if Sophia would like a cup of tea or some broth but Sophia said that she wouldn't. 'No,' said William grumpily. 'She wants to go to bed and groan and keep me awake all night as she did last night; but she shall not keep me awake tonight.'

The Ockold's son, Thomas, and daughter-in-law, Ellen, visited later that evening and found Sophia sitting on a bench, her head resting on the kitchen table, with William worriedly making her a cup of tea. Thomas believed that his seventy-three-year-old mother had suffered a stroke. She was unable to hold her head upright and Thomas eventually had to support her head and pour her tea down her throat. Ellen made up a clean bed for her mother-in-law, after which Thomas and Ellen together carried her upstairs, undressed her and put her to bed.

At ten past three in the morning of 8 November, Constable Daniel Hutchings was walking his regular beat around Oldbury when he passed the Ockold's cottage. He could hear groaning, cursing and swearing coming from inside and clearly heard a man's voice saying, 'You damned old cat! You are very bad I dare say but I never knew you when you were good.' Hutchings also made out the words 'Damn your eyes! If you don't come downstairs I will...', but didn't catch the rest of the threat.

Hutchings waited outside the cottage for some time, listening to the commotion from within, but didn't feel that it was his place to interfere, particularly as he had heard William and Sophia arguing and cursing at each other many times before as he passed their home. He didn't continue on his beat until five minutes to four, by which time things had quietened down.

On the morning of 8 November, Maria came back to check on Sophia and found William sitting at the table sewing. 'How is grandmother this morning?' she asked him.

'I don't know,' replied William.

'Where is she?' asked Maria.

'I don't know,' said William again.

Surprised by his answers, Maria looked at William and noticed for the first time that his hand was bruised and stained with blood. When she asked him how he had hurt his hand, William thought for a moment then told Maria, 'It's from giving her a punch in the mouth.'

Maria was appalled, telling William that Sophia was ill enough already without being punched and asking him why on earth he had hit his wife.

'For going off and getting drunk with that Jack Hadley,' answered William. When Maria reasoned that Sophia was barely capable of walking, yet alone going out drinking, William told her that Sophia had not been ill but blind drunk.

'Where is she?' Maria asked again and predictably William answered 'I don't know.'

'Is she in bed?' persisted Maria.

'I don't know.'

At that, Maria decided to look for herself and walked towards the stairs.

'You bain't a-going upstairs,' William told her, but Maria ignored him and went anyway. She found Sophia Ockold lying dead on the landing.

Maria rounded on William telling him, 'You have killed that old woman.'

'Her ain't dead, is her?' asked William in apparent disbelief. 'Her's only asleep.'

'She'll never wake again,' Maria told him before running out of the house to fetch her employer, Mrs Woodall.

By the time Mrs Woodall and Maria returned, William was upstairs and the two women could hear the sound of something heavy being dragged across the floor. When William came downstairs again, his hands were bloody and he went straight into the pantry to wash them. He then stood quietly in the chimney corner, waiting for the police to arrive.

Constable Samuel Simmons and Mr Thomas Cooper, a local surgeon, arrived almost simultaneously, by which time Sophia was lying in her bed. While Cooper pronounced Mrs Ockold dead, after viewing her body, Constable Simmons arrested William.

'You naughty old man – what could you have been thinking of to serve the old woman like that?' asked Simmons.

'I did not do it wilfully,' replied William, later saying, 'I only struck her once.'

Taken to the police station, William was examined and found to have large quantities of blood on his shirt and trousers, as well as an abrasion on the forefinger of his right hand. 'I did that against her teeth,' he told Constable Simmons then repeated his story about his wife getting drunk with Jack Hadley on the previous day. He went on to say that he had been bound all his life. 'First, I was bound to my mother and father, then I was bound to my master and for fifty years I have been bound to my wife and now, thank God, I'm free and I would not now have the brightest woman as ever wore a head.'

Mr Cooper later conducted a post-mortem examination on Sophia Ockold, who he had been treating for kidney disease at the time of her death. He found several bruises of varying ages all over her body and recent abrasions on her left cheek, left arm and both legs. On her right cheek was a deep cut and the cheekbone beneath it was fractured. She had bled heavily from her nose.

Once Cooper opened Sophia's skull, the cause of her death was obvious. Sophia had a ruptured blood vessel in her brain that had caused a large blood clot to form, which Cooper removed, along with about 1oz of liquid blood. The muscle in her right temple had been pulped and now bore a strong resemblance to a piece of liver.

Cooper attributed Sophia's death to an act of extreme violence, saying that he did not believe that a fall could have caused such injuries, even if the deceased had fallen face first onto an object, unless she had fallen onto it from a great height. He discounted a fall downstairs, since the staircase at the cottage was round, making it impossible to fall from top to bottom without striking a wall after only a short distance.

Sophia had an abscess on her kidneys and slight congestion of her lungs but was otherwise a healthy old woman. Cooper also noted that she had no teeth and that he had found no traces of either beer or spirits during his examination.

A search of the Ockold's cottage revealed a large clump of grey hair at the bottom of the stairs, along with a few spots of blood, and there were blood smears on the walls at the sides of the stairs. The police also found half of a recently broken mop handle, which was stained with blood. They took it to Mr Cooper, who agreed with them that being struck with it might well have caused Sophia's injuries. Curiously, the police only ever found half of the mop handle at the cottage and were unable to find the other half.

Charged with the wilful murder of his wife, William Ockold continued to insist that he had not done it wilfully. Nevertheless, the coroner's jury at Sophia's inquest recorded a verdict of wilful murder against him and he was committed to stand trial at the next Worcester Assizes.

The expected opening of the trial was delayed for one day since Ellen Ockold, who was considered to be a key witness, had recently given birth to a baby. In the event, she was still not considered well enough to attend when the trial began and, although she gave a deposition of her account of the night before her mother-in-law's murder, the counsel for the defence, Mr Benson, objected to its inclusion and his objection was upheld.

Thus, the court heard only from Thomas Ockold, Maria Grazebrook, her employer Lavinia Woodall, and PCs Hutchings and Simmons. Mr Cooper testified about the results of the post-mortem examination, after which Mr Richards and Mr Griffiths, the counsels for the prosecution, called three surprise witnesses.

The first of these was pub landlady Elizabeth James, who kept the Hope and Anchor pub on the Halesowen road. It was at this public house that, according to William, Sophia had become so drunk in the company of Jack Hadley that she had been quite unable to find her way home again and, when she finally did get home, was completely incapable of standing up. Mrs James knew both of the Ockolds, as well as Jack Hadley, and swore that none of the three were at her premises on the day in question.

Next to take the stand was John 'Jack' Hadley. He told the court that he had known the Ockolds for forty years. He had been told that Sophia was unwell and had called at the Ockold's cottage on 7 November to find out how she was, staying for about ten minutes. William Ockold had been present throughout Hadley's entire visit and Hadley insisted that he had not been drinking with Sophia that day and in fact had never been out drinking with her.

The third witness was a labourer named Jeremiah Bradley, who stabled his horses about 10 yards from the Ockolds' home. At four o'clock on the morning of 8 November, he had heard William Ockold using what he described as 'very bad language' towards his wife. Bradley had listened at the Ockold's door to hear Sophia begging, 'Oh, Bill, don't kill me, for my head is ready to split,' a phrase she repeated three or four times.

Bradley told the court that he eventually left because he couldn't stand to hear such 'blackguard language'. He had often heard the couple rowing before but had never heard such terrible cursing. In answer to a question from the defence counsel, he said that it had not occurred to him to intervene.

At this, the prosecution rested, opening the floor for counsel for the defence. Mr Benson asked the jury for their indulgences to the suggestions that he was about to make on behalf of 'this unfortunate old man' and begged them not to be swayed by the 'thrilling tale of horror' that his learned friend the counsel for the prosecution had laid before them. Benson then proceeded to revisit the facts of the case in great detail, challenging every one of them.

Where was the motive for the murder of Sophia Ockold, he asked the jury? They had heard from witnesses in court that Sophia helped William with his tailoring work, probably doing at least half of it, so consequently her death would deprive William of his livelihood. If William had killed Sophia, why did he not try to conceal his deeds? Why did he allow Maria Grazebrook to go upstairs if he knew that she would find Sophia's battered body there?

If Sophia had been attacked downstairs, as the blood and hair at the bottom of the stairs might suggest, how did she then get upstairs? Her son and Maria Grazebrook had both testified that she was unable to walk and Thomas had said that it required both him and his wife together to carry his mother up to bed. Could a frail, wretched old man like his client conceivably have carried his wife upstairs alone?

Benson told the jury that William Ockold strenuously denied killing his wife. In all probability, there had been a brief struggle upstairs and William had hit Sophia in a moment of passion and had gone downstairs in complete ignorance of the terrible consequences of his actions. When Maria Grazebrook arrived at the house, William was sitting calmly at the table sewing – could he possibly have been that composed knowing that he had just killed his wife? Thomas had seen his mother only hours before her death and had believed that she had suffered a stroke. Surely, at the very worst, all that the jury could convict his client of was manslaughter.

Mr Justice Mellor then summed up the case for the jury. The killing of one person by another, he explained, was murder, unless there were verifiable circumstances that justified a reduction of the charge to manslaughter. Mellor said that he knew of only one instance where a case of murder could be reduced to manslaughter where there was no provocation or struggle between the killer and the victim beyond mere words and that was when a man found his wife in the act of adultery and immediately killed her paramour.

In arriving at their verdict, the jury must give due consideration to the question of provocation and, if they believed that there had been a physical struggle between Sophia and William Ockold immediately before her death then a verdict of manslaughter might be appropriate in this case. However, if they believed that the physical violence came entirely from William, then the proper verdict was one of murder. The jury must decide if there had been any act of violence on Sophia's part.

The judge urged the jury not to be swayed by pity for the defendant on account of his age but also warned them not to give vent to any feelings of indignation that they might harbour over the violent death of an elderly lady.

The jury retired for more than an hour, obviously giving the case their most careful consideration, before returning with a verdict of 'Guilty of Wilful Murder' against William Ockold. The foreman of the jury informed the judge that their verdict came with a recommendation of mercy for the prisoner on account of his age and previous good character.

Mr Justice Mellor then addressed William Ockold, telling him that it was a pity that, at his advanced stage of life, he should be convicted of such a crime against the wife he had sworn to love and cherish. Promising to forward the jury's recommendations to the proper quarter, he then pronounced sentence of death on the accused, who accepted his fate with no perceptible trace of emotion.

In the days prior to his execution, Ockold outwardly maintained the same indifference to his situation. However, on receiving a letter from his daughter, in which she asked him why he was showing no emotion at the death of his wife, he told her that even if he wasn't showing it, he might be feeling it. His son, Thomas, visited him and begged his father to tell him the truth about his mother's death. William continued to insist that he hadn't killed Sophia. He told Thomas that he and Sophia had argued because she wouldn't stay in bed and he had hit her once in the mouth and then gone downstairs. Later, he had heard a loud thump and, on going upstairs, found Sophia lying on the landing, her arms twitching, having fallen out of bed.

'It was not from anything she had from me that she died,' he told Thomas.

The inhabitants of Oldbury petitioned the Home Secretary for a reprieve, but received a reply stating that Sir George Grey did not see sufficient reason to interfere with the course of justice. Other people also petitioned the Home Secretary on Ockold's behalf, including the city magistrates of Worcester and the members of the coroner's jury on whose verdict Ockold had been sent for trial. However, all the petitions were in vain and Ockold went to the gallows on 2 January 1863.

The crowd who assembled outside the jail to view the execution was considerably smaller than might have been expected, probably due to a night of torrential rain and gale force wind. Still, between 4,000 and 5,000 people gathered to watch the spectacle, many of them women and children. They saw Ockold walking firmly and resolutely to the gallows and only those who were closest saw the tears trickling slowly down his cheeks as he faced his death. Having shaken hands with Calcraft, the executioner, William Ockold said, 'I suppose I'm going now.'

He appeared to die as soon as the drop fell from beneath his feet and it was only when his body was cut down that it was realised that the rope had cut through one side of his frail neck.

After the execution, Calcraft left Worcester immediately to carry out another 'job' in Liverpool. The local newspaper of the time reported that, prior to the execution, a hoax letter had been sent to the proprietor of a hotel in the city. Headed 'Old Bailey, London Dec 31 1862' it asked that a strictly quiet bedroom and sitting room be reserved for the night before the execution. Signed J. Calcraft, the letter instructed the hotelier not to mention the name of his guest to any soul but to send a cab to meet the last train from London. The local paper called the hoaxer 'some silly fellow who ought to be whipped with Calcraft's cord for his pains.' The newspaper also reported that morbidly curious souvenir hunters had besieged the cottage in which the murder was committed. It had been 'in a tumbledown state' when Ockold had left it but now all the windows had been stoned and the front door forced off its hinges. In a short time, predicted the newspaper, all that will remain is the ground on which it is built and the bare walls. One wonders what Mr Hackett, the owner of the property, thought about such wanton destruction.

Note: The contemporary newspaper accounts of the murder mention a Constable Simmons and a Sergeant Simmonds. It is not clear whether these are two different police officers or variations of the name and rank of the same man. It is also stated that William and Sophia used the surname Hooker at times, as well as Ockold.

11

'SOMEBODY OUGHT TO MIND HIM'

Holt Fleet, 1864

At sixty-two years old, John Butler was the oldest serving employee of the Severn Improvement Commissioners, working as the lock keeper at Holt Fleet, about 6 miles from Worcester. Until four years previously his wife, Frances, had assisted him with his duties, but she had died and, soon after her death, he had employed a housekeeper, Catherine Gulliver. However, before long, Catherine was doing much more than just keeping house for John Butler. The couple lived as man and wife in the lock keeper's cottage, although their relationship was often punctuated by arguments, usually triggered by Butler's jealousy.

On 13 August 1864, Catherine went to a shop near to the lock and bought some groceries. While there, she complained bitterly to Mrs Taylor, the shopkeeper, about Butler's behaviour, saying, 'Somebody ought to mind him.' Mrs Taylor suggested that she wrote to the surgeon, Mr Busigny, about Butler and offered her a pen and some paper, but Catherine declined the offer.

From the shop, Catherine went to a nearby pub, where she drank a glass of beer and purchased some more to take home with her. She made no complaint about Butler at the pub, seeming very cheerful, but by eleven o'clock that night she was back at the pub complaining that Butler had ripped off her bonnet and locked her out of their cottage.

Mrs Green, the pub landlady, offered her a bed for the night, but Catherine told her that she would go home, saying that Butler would no doubt let her in again once his temper had cooled down. Mrs Green told her that she would sit up until midnight and that if Catherine couldn't get into the house or if Butler mistreated her, then she was to come straight back to the pub. When there was no sign of Catherine, Mrs Green assumed that the quarrel had blown over and thought no more about it.

The lock keeper's cottage at Holt Fleet. (© N. Sly, 2008)

Having left the pub, Catherine was seen walking towards the lock by a Mr Henry Thrupp, who wished her 'Goodnight.' Shortly afterwards, Mrs Green's daughter, Ann, heard three short screams coming from that direction and the cries were also heard by the under lock keeper, John Harris, and his wife, Elizabeth, who lived in the cottage next door to John Butler's home. The Harris's described the sounds as somebody 'bleating like a sheep' or saying 'whaa, whaa'. Nobody took any particular notice of the cries, since Butler and his housekeeper frequently fought and argued.

Early the following morning, a Sunday, John Butler was seen to raise the lock, as if to allow something to escape, all the while looking furtively around him to see if anybody was watching. Later that day, Elizabeth Harris asked him about the strange noises that she and her husband had heard during the previous night.

'Was it Mrs Gulliver?' she asked and Butler said that it was. He told Elizabeth that, at around midnight, he had been in bed when Mrs Gulliver had come home drunk. She had thrown the groceries she had bought all over the house then stormed off in a fit of temper. Later that day, Mrs Harris asked Butler if Catherine had arrived home yet. Butler told her that she hadn't but that he supposed she would be back in a day or two. He complained of having no hot water to shave with, since Catherine had not been around to light the fire and asked Elizabeth if she could let him have some.

Over the next couple of days, several people asked after Catherine Gulliver and all were given the same reply. Butler supposed that she had gone to visit friends in Worcester, something she had talked of doing, and he expected that she would be back in a couple of days. People began to grow uneasy about Catherine, since she

The lock at Holt Fleet. (© N. Sly, 2008)

was not known to have any friends in the area and eventually pub landlord Samuel Green voiced his concerns to Butler, telling him that he believed that Catherine was in the river and suggesting that Butler should look for her if he didn't want to be blamed for her disappearance. Butler made no reply beyond a heavy sigh.

The rumours of Catherine Gulliver's disappearance eventually reached the ears of the parish vicar, Revd John Gurney Rogers. Rogers was very familiar with the fiery relationship between Butler and his housekeeper, as Catherine had complained to him in the past about Butler's treatment of her. He confronted John Butler, who told him that he was very poorly, but refused to elaborate on the whereabouts of his housekeeper, answering the vicar's questions only with vague grunts and sighs. Rogers left Butler and went straight to the police with his suspicions.

Sergeant Matthews was also familiar with Catherine and John's fighting as, less than two months before her disappearance Catherine had made a complaint to him about John's violence towards her, saying he had threatened to drown her. Matthews had visited Butler and warned him about his conduct, at which Butler promised that it would never be repeated. Matthews had then advised Catherine to apply for a warrant from the magistrates, but, the next day, she had returned to see the policeman, telling him that she wished the complaint to go no further as there was something between her and Butler 'that everybody did not know about.' Now, with Catherine missing, Matthews ordered the river to be dragged and, on 17 August, the fully-clothed body of a woman was pulled from the water, close to the lock.

The River Severn from Holt Fleet, 1913. (Author's collection)

Surgeon Busigny was sent for. He knew Catherine Gulliver and was instantly able to positively identify the body as hers.

Catherine had unmistakeable marks of violence on her face. Her lower jaw was swollen and discoloured, as if from a punch. She had a walnut-sized lump on her forehead and a black eye.

Busigny later conducted a post-mortem examination on the body of Catherine Gulliver, at which he found little of note, except for congestion of the lungs. He was able to state with some certainty that she had suffered the black eye before her death, although he was unsure whether the other two wounds on her face had occurred before or after death. His belief was that Catherine had been stunned by the blow on her forehead and then thrown into the water, but he could find no traces of water in her lungs and could not state whether or not she had breathed after her immersion in the water.

Butler was promptly arrested and charged with Catherine Gulliver's wilful murder. His only response to the charge was to say dolefully, 'Oh, dear.' Taken to the police station, all he said in answer to the questions put to him was, 'Do you think there will be rain tonight?'

Butler appeared at the Winter Assizes at Worcester on 15 December 1864, before Mr Justice Byles. Mr Richards and Mr J.G. Watkins prosecuted the case, while Mr Motteram defended.

The prosecution called a number of witnesses to tell the court their version of the events immediately preceding the discovery of Catherine's body in the river.

Many also testified about the turbulent relationship between the forty-four-year-old housekeeper and John Butler. When Mr Busigny testified, the counsel for the defence subjected him to a rigorous cross-examination, which lasted for just over an hour.

Mr Motteram wanted it made absolutely clear to the court which of Catherine Gulliver's injuries had been caused before her death and which after; something that Mr Busigny was unable to do. Referring to the definitive book on the subject at the time, *Dr Taylor's Medical Jurisprudence*, he gave his opinion that the cause of Mrs Gulliver's death had been an injury arising from concussion and immersion in the water, producing immediate suffocation. He still believed that Catherine's black eye had occurred before her death and most probably the bump on her forehead too, which would have left her stunned or even unconscious. However, he could not rule out the theory that she had fallen into the water and hit a hard object, or that one of the numerous barges and boats that used the river had not struck her at some point while she was in the water. Interestingly, given that she was supposed to have drunk a glass of beer at the pub shortly before her death, Mr Busigny had found no trace of beer in her stomach, just a small amount of undigested food.

Once all the witnesses had been heard, the prosecution rested and Mr Motteram began his defence of John Butler. He began by telling the court of Butler's previous good character and of his more-than-twenty-year service for the same company, a company that held him in very high regard. (This was not strictly true, as Butler's supervisor had already testified that, although Butler was a long-serving and highly valued employee, he had been a little 'strange' since his wife had died and the company was keen for him to retire.)

No evidence had been produced to show that any kind of 'improper intimacy' existed between the accused and the victim and it was purely on this basis that the jury must arrive at their verdict. They should not make other assumptions.

Motteram then addressed the medical evidence, telling the jury that he would have been far happier had Mr Busigny studied his subject before venturing a hasty opinion. The court had no real evidence as to the manner in which Catherine Gulliver met her death and yet they were being asked to make decisions on the life and death of the defendant solely on the opinion of one man. Furthermore, the prosecution had not managed to establish any motive whatsoever for John Butler to kill his housekeeper – had he wished to get rid of her, all he had to do was give her a month's wages and send her packing.

The surgeon was the key witness, on whose testimony the jury were being asked to '...take upon themselves the awful responsibility of hurtling into eternity a grey-headed old man.' That surgeon had given his opinion that the deceased did not die from drowning but had received a mortal blow before being put into the water. He had put forward opinions that he was unable to back up with scientific knowledge and, because of this, the jury could not even be certain that a murder had been committed. Mrs Gulliver could have stumbled into the water accidentally or have deliberately thrown herself into the river, with the intention of drowning herself. Calling the prosecution witnesses 'busy bodies' Motteram remarked that it was a pity that none of them had thought to interfere when they had first heard a woman's screams.

There was, concluded Motteram, simply no case to answer as, even if Catherine Gulliver had been murdered, rather than died by accident or by her own intention, there was nothing whatsoever to suggest that John Butler was her killer. Indeed, such evidence as there was more strongly suggested an accidental death.

After the judge's summary, the jury retired for an hour before returning with a verdict of 'Guilty of Wilful Murder' against John Butler. Mr Justice Byles expressed his approval of the verdict and pronounced the death sentence on the prisoner.

While Butler awaited his sentence at Worcester Prison, a number of inhabitants of Worcester convened an urgent meeting in the Guildhall with a view to petitioning the Home Secretary for a reprieve for the condemned man. Among those who attended were Mr Williams, an engineer for the Severn Navigation Commissioners; the coroner, Mr Rea; the attorney, Mr Clutterbuck; and Aldermen Lea, Webb, Wood and Hill.

All felt that, while they could not state whether Butler was guilty or not, the trial had raised sufficient doubts on the matter to concern them. Accordingly, a memorial was composed, which, after stating the known facts of the case, continued:

> That many of your memorialists were present at the trial of the prisoner and heard the whole of the evidence against him and for him, and were unable to concur in the verdict of the jury, notwithstanding it met with the approbation of the judge who tried the prisoner. That, in the judgement of your memorialists, such evidence did not exclude the probability that the deceased might have come by her death by voluntary or accidental drowning. Your memorialists respectfully submit that there is grave and serious doubt upon the propriety of this prisoner's conviction and that the mind of society is entitled to be relieved from the dread apprehension that afflicts it while the majesty of the law is being vindicated to a man, a sight more fearful in the eyes of God may be enacted in the mistaken sacrifice of another human life. Your memorialists, therefore, humbly pray that the recommendation by the jury of the prisoner to the merciful consideration of the Court may be brought under the gracious consideration of the Crown and the life of the convict be spared. [*sic*]

By the close of the meeting, the petition had been signed by 100 people and it was to attract many more signatures before it was finally despatched to the then Home Secretary, Sir George Grey. Although the committee apparently didn't hold out much hope for the success of their appeal, there is no record of Butler's execution.

12

'EACH MUST TAKE CARE OF HIMSELF'

Bromsgrove, 1872

'Marry in haste, repent at leisure' goes the old saying and twenty-five-year-old Maria Holmes was certainly doing just that. She and her husband, Charles, had a four-year-old crippled son – the reason for their hasty marriage four years earlier – and it was evident that Charles, who was some years older than his wife, resented both Maria and the boy. Unfortunately for Maria, her husband frequently expressed his resentment with his fists, especially when he had been drinking, which was a regular occurrence.

On 7 March 1872, Maria was forced to fetch Charles from the public house, where he had been fighting with another man. Later that evening, a neighbour heard Maria and the child sobbing bitterly in the garden of their cottage near Bromsgrove. When the neighbour asked her what the matter was, Maria replied that Charles had tried to throttle her.

'She's a damned liar!' Charles growled, at which Maria walked off and sat down in the road outside the cottage.

Charles followed and ordered her to go back into the house and make his supper. Maria refused point blank to do so, telling her husband that if she could get a policeman, she would have him arrested. Charles again asked her to get his supper and once more she refused, at which Charles told her that, if she did not, he would make her fit for a coffin. At that, Maria reluctantly went indoors, but she had obviously had enough of Charles's beatings and bullying ways as, on the following day, she left him, turning up on her mother's doorstep in the morning with her child in her arms.

Charles was furious. As soon as he found Maria gone, he stormed round to her mother's house and demanded that his wife and son return home immediately.

Maria refused and, after a brief argument, Charles went home alone, although he was back shortly afterwards, again ordering her to come home.

Again, Maria refused and once more Charles was forced to go home without her although he was soon back, pressing Maria to go back with him. Maria ignored his demands and walked upstairs without speaking, at which he threatened her, 'I will only come back once more...'

His fourth visit of the day was at half-past four in the afternoon. Maria answered her mother's front door with her son in her arms and again tried to ignore his ranting and raving at her to return, although she did take a pair of shoes he had brought for her from home. However, having turned her back on him, she was just about to walk away when he asked his son, 'Will you have a penny?'

The little boy eagerly held out his hand for the coin and Maria stopped to allow him to take it. As she did, Charles took a razor from his coat pocket and swiftly drew it across her throat from ear to ear. Maria dropped her child and staggered to the middle of the room, blood gushing from her throat. She collapsed moments later in front of her horrified mother, dead from loss of blood almost before she hit the ground. Charles calmly told his mother-in-law, 'Each must take care of himself,' and then left.

He went from his mother-in-law's home to the New Rose and Crown Inn then walked a few miles to his brother's home, where he made a half-hearted attempt to cut his own throat. The wound was only superficial and, when the police arrived to arrest him later that evening, he was well enough to accompany them to the police station, where he was charged with the wilful murder of his wife. He immediately

Kidderminster Road, Bromsgrove. (Author's collection)

admitted killing Maria, saying that he wouldn't have done it had she been willing to come home with him.

Appearing before magistrates, he continued to admit his guilt and was committed to stand trial at the next Worcester Assizes. Sadly, Maria's mother, Mrs James, had been so affected by the shock of seeing her daughter so brutally slain before her eyes that she died before Holmes could be brought to trial.

By the time his trial opened on 22 July 1872, he had been persuaded to plead 'Not Guilty'. Mr Jelf and Mr Clay, the counsels for the prosecution, opened the proceedings by outlining the events of 7 and 8 March and it was then left to Mr Motteram and Mr Young to try and defend Holmes.

Given his confession, it was evident to all that he had killed his wife, even without the testimony of the late Mrs James, who had appeared at the magistrate's court as an eyewitness to the murder. Thus, all Motteram could do was to suggest to the jury that his client should be convicted of the lesser offence of manslaughter, arguing that the conduct of Maria Holmes before her death had amounted to provocation and was, in the eyes of the law, sufficiently provoking to merit a reduction in the charge.

The presiding judge, Mr Justice Grove, summed up the case for the jury and explaining the necessary amount of provocation required in order to reduce an offence from murder to manslaughter. Generally there are four conditions that must be fulfilled to warrant the reduction – the provocation must cause rage or fear in a reasonable person, the defendant must have actually been provoked, there should not be a sufficient time period between the provocation and the killing as to permit a reasonable person to cool off, and the defendant should not have cooled off during that period. Having explained the legal details, Mr Justice Grove outlined the facts of the case then left the jury to see if they could see how Charles Holmes might have been provoked into killing his wife.

The jury didn't even feel the need to retire to consider their verdict, pronouncing Charles Holmes 'Guilty'. Holmes struggled briefly with warders in the dock as the judge put on the black cap, then quickly pulled himself together and listened impassively as the sentence of death was passed upon him.

Confined in Worcester County Prison awaiting his execution, Charles Holmes showed extreme remorse for killing his wife and acknowledged that his sentence was fair and just. Nevertheless, a letter was sent to the then Home Secretary, requesting that Holmes's death sentence should be reconsidered. Mr Bruce declined to interfere with the course of justice and, on 12 August 1872, thirty-eight-year-old Charles Holmes was executed by William Calcraft. It was the first ever private hanging to be held at Worcester but, even so, a crowd of between 400 and 500 people assembled outside the prison to see the customary black flag hoisted over the building.

13

'IF EVER I WAS TO MEET WITH HIM I SHOULD BE A MATCH FOR HIM'

Alvechurch, 1885

At around half-past eight on the morning of 28 February 1885, farmer John Twigg was walking to work along Eagle Street Lane, when he spotted a walking stick lying abandoned in the middle of the road. He picked it up and walked on but, before long, he was to make a far more shocking find on the quiet country lane near Alvechurch. As he rounded a slight bend about 60 yards further along the road, he came across the body of a uniformed policeman lying on his back, at right angles to the hedgerow. Twigg immediately recognised the dead man as Constable James Davies, who was stationed at Beoley. Although it was obvious to Twigg that Davies was dead, he bent to put his hand on the constable's forehead, finding it stone cold. As he did, he noticed two distinct footprints, one on either side of the man's head.

Twigg went to the nearest farm, which was occupied by the Newbold family, and a messenger was sent on horseback to the police station at Alvechurch. While waiting for the police to arrive, Twigg went back to the body, where he realised for the first time that there were trails of clear footprints leading to and from where the body lay.

Two sets of footprints led from the direction of Weatheroak Hill. One set was made by a set of nailed boots, identical to those worn by the dead policeman. The other was larger and had an unusual shape, being wide in the middle with a distinctly pointed toe. From the body, just the strangely shaped prints led off towards Beoley.

Thinking quickly, Twigg broke some branches of the hedge and laid them over the footprints nearest the body to preserve them. There were signs of a struggle having taken place where the policeman had fallen and another about 20 yards away.

The Alvechurch police were soon on the scene, along with surgeon Mr J.P. Gaunt, who initially examined the body where it lay. The man's overcoat and uniform jacket were open, as was his waistcoat and his helmet lay on the ground by his left foot, his policemen's staff by his right. His police whistle was found some distance away from the body.

Gaunt found that, where the body was covered with clothing, it was still warm. Davies had a long cut on his face, crossing his right cheek from chin to ear. There was a deep stab wound in the right-hand side of his neck, which was disguised by a quantity of whitish foam. When Gaunt wiped the foam away, he could see that the policeman's throat had also been deeply slashed, the cut being about 3½in long. Davies had obviously fought his murderer valiantly, as two fingers on his right hand and one on his left were almost severed and there was a large cut on one of his thumbs. There was a quantity of hair clutched in Davies' hands, which seemed to resemble hair from his own whiskers, and a number of feathers scattered around the body.

The body was eventually removed to a nearby barn to enable the surgeon to examine it more closely. Gaunt determined the cause of death to be blood loss, mainly from the severed jugular vein and carotid artery on the left-hand side of Davies' throat. It was also noted that one of Davies' pockets had been cut away and that the silver watch and chain that he habitually carried were missing.

Alvechurch. (© N. Sly, 2008)

It was known that thirty-three-year-old Davies, who left a wife and four young children, had started his shift at ten o'clock the previous evening. He had kept a planned rendezvous with Constable Whitehouse, the Wythall policeman, at one o'clock in the morning and the two officers had parted company at just after two o'clock. While they were together, they had heard the clock at the Rose and Crown public house striking two, at which both men had checked their watches. Constable Davies found that his watch had stopped ten minutes earlier, so he reset and wound it.

After his meeting with Constable Whitehouse, Davies had walked off alone towards Weatheroak Hill Farm. He was scheduled to meet the Alvechurch policeman at Rowney Green at four o'clock but unfortunately that policeman had been taken ill and was at home in bed at the time of the meeting. Hence, nobody missed Davies or realised that he was in trouble.

While the police were at the scene of the murder, they were informed that a number of hens had been stolen from Weatheroak Hill Farm during the previous night. When they went to investigate the theft, Superintendent Jeffrey from Bromsgrove and Sergeant Long from Redditch noticed a number of footprints in the muddy farmyard, which seemed identical to those found around Davies' body. Jeffrey tracked the prints across two fields and for a few yards along Eagle Street Lane. There, passing traffic had obliterated them but, as Jeffrey continued walking towards the scene of the murder, the footprints resumed, now joined by a second set of footprints made by nailed boots. It was beginning to look as though Davies

The grave of PC James Davies. (© N. Sly, 2008)

had intercepted the poultry thief, placed him under arrest and was escorting him to the police station when the thief had attacked and killed him. The Newbold family told the police that they had not heard any cries for help, although their dog had begun barking fiercely at between half-past three and four o'clock in the morning, most probably at the time that the murder was taking place.

Six birds had been stolen in total – two light brown, two white and two dark coloured. It was not known whether the thief had taken them away alive or killed them on the farm, so the police appealed through the local newspaper for anyone who had recently bought one or more of the six fowls, alive or dead, to contact them. They also asked for any information on Davies' missing watch, publishing the maker's name and the serial number.

Superintendent Jeffrey sent telegrams to all of the police divisions in the area, describing the murder and when Superintendent Tyler of King's Heath received his telegram it struck a chord. In his office, he had a photograph of Moses Shrimpton, a known fowl-stealer, who had only recently been released from prison. Tyler took the photograph to detectives in Moor Street, Birmingham and Detective Inspector Stroud instantly recognised the man as one he currently had under observation, suspected of stealing poultry.

Tyler went off in search of Shrimpton and, at ten o'clock at night on 1 March, he and Stroud found him outside a liquor store. They watched their quarry surreptitiously from the shadows, until Shrimpton entered a house in Bartholomew Street.

Tyler confronted Shrimpton in a third-floor room, where he had retired to bed with his common-law wife, Mary Morton. When the policemen barged into the room, Shrimpton leaped out of bed saying, 'Hallo, what's up?' at which Stroud arrested him on suspicion of the murder of Constable Davies. Shrimpton said nothing when he was charged but Mary was a little more vocal. Told that she too was under arrest, she asked the policemen, 'What for? I have done nothing.' The couple's room was searched and a bloodstained pillowcase was found, in which there was a feather and some very fresh fowl dung. A bucket and bowl of reddish-coloured water were also found, at the bottom of which were layers of sand, similar in appearance to the soil at the site of the murder.

Shrimpton and Mary Morton were taken to the police station, where it was noted that Shrimpton had a number of fresh wounds on his forehead and close to his left ear, which were oozing watery pus. Plasters had been applied to some of the wounds and, when asked by the police how he had come by his injuries, Shrimpton replied that he had fallen over about a week earlier while drunk.

When Mary Morton was searched, a pocketknife was found in her dress pocket. The knife, which appeared to have been recently washed, had reddish clay soil embedded in a crevice in the handle, as well as what looked like a bloodstain at the base of the blade. Moses Shrimpton admitted that the knife was his.

Shrimpton's clothes and boots were seized and examined. Even though the clothes seemed to have been recently washed, the sleeve of his greatcoat was saturated in blood and the coat was stained with the same reddish clay as the knife. Inside the coat was a large 'poacher's pocket', extending from the breast to the bottom hem. The police found feathers, mud and fresh chicken droppings in this pocket, along with spots of blood on the inside of Shrimpton's waistcoat and shirt and on a cardigan jacket. Blood was also found at the top of his right-hand trouser pocket. There were two distinct indentations in Shrimpton's felt hat, one of which exactly corresponded in position with the location of the wound on his forehead.

Shrimpton's boots had been recently washed and greased, as was evidenced by the presence of a greasy rag on the mantelpiece of his room at Bartholomew Street. The boots were taken to the scene of the murder and compared with the prints found there. They proved to be a perfect match, even down to a patch on the sole of the right boot, near to the heel. The clothes were sent to Home Office analyst Dr Stevenson, in London, for closer examination, along with the knife and some samples of the soil taken from the scene of the murder.

On 2 March, Moses Shrimpton was charged with stealing six fowls belonging to Mr Fisher on 27 February and with the murder of Constable James Davies on 28 February. Mary Morton was charged with being an accessory after the fact to both the theft and the murder. Both Shrimpton and Morton protested their innocence, Shrimpton asking for bail (which was not surprisingly refused) and Mary Morton saying, 'As true as God's in heaven, I knew nothing about it until you came and took us on Saturday.' However, when she was additionally charged on the following day with being an accessory to the theft of Constable Davies' watch, she evidently decided that it was in her best interests to make a statement.

She told the police that on Friday 27 February, she had been at her work as a charwoman until about six o'clock, after which she had stayed at home all night doing her washing. She had seen Moses at their home at about a quarter past six, but since the couple had rowed on the previous day, he had not spoken to her at all but had left the house in a sulk.

She had next seen him on the following morning at about ten o'clock when she had remarked to him, 'How ill you look. What's the matter?'

Moses told her that he had fallen over and hit his head on a kerbstone. Mary went out to buy some sticking plaster and dressed the wounds on his forehead, after which he had eaten some breakfast. She then asked him for money but he told her that he had none until Monday. He pulled a watch and chain out of his coat pocket and told Mary that he had spent all his money buying it. She asked him how much he had paid for it, to which he answered, 'Not much, you may be sure,' telling her that she wouldn't know the person he had purchased it from.

He suggested that they take the watch to Mary's employer, Mrs Facer, to see if she would buy it from them. Minutes later, Moses went out, leaving the watch and chain in the room. Mary picked it up and took it to the home of Mr and Mrs Facer, where she found Moses already waiting for her.

'I hear you have a watch to show me?' said Mrs Facer. She inspected the watch that Mary pulled from the bosom of her dress then told Mary that she already had a similar one, pointing to a watch on the mantelpiece. Mary asked for the loan of 2s against the watch but Mrs Facer was not interested and eventually left the room. As soon as she did so, Moses turned to Mary and, shaking his fist at her to emphasize his point, insisted, 'You must leave it here. I tell you, you must leave it here.' When Mrs Facer returned, she was eventually persuaded to give Mary 1s against the watch.

Mary told the police that she had asked Moses why he had been so insistent that the watch was left with Mrs Facer and he told her that he was concerned that there was something 'not quite right' about it and that the man he had bought it from had not come about it honestly. It was best out of their house for the time being.

From the Facer's house, Moses and Mary had gone to a pub, where they had drunk beer and eaten bread and cheese. Moses had given Mary his knife to cut her cheese and, when she had finished using it, she had unthinkingly slipped it into her dress pocket.

When the police went to the Facer's home in search of the watch, they discovered that Mr Facer, who worked as a maltster, had already disposed of the watch by throwing it into a malt kiln at work. The police went to his place of work and had the kiln fire damped down, carefully searching the ashes, but no trace of the watch was ever found. They promptly charged George Facer with being an accessory to murder after the fact, although the case against him was later dismissed at the magistrate's court.

The fowls stolen from the farm had now been found, all dead. Two lay in a watercourse on a footpath leading to Seechem Farm, where the footprints from the murder scene had led. Some days later, the bodies of a further four birds were found among some thorn bushes in a deep pit in a field at the farm and, unexpectedly, the body of a seventh bird was found close by. The police had also identified the walking stick found by Mr Twigg a few yards from the body as being one belonging to Moses Shrimpton.

Meanwhile, Shrimpton told the police that, on the night of the murder, he had been hunting rabbits alone at Yardley and insisted that he had not been to Worcestershire for more than twelve months.

Moses and Mary were kept separately in custody at Winson Green Prison in Birmingham, while the police continued with their investigations. They were brought together for the first time since their arrest to attend the inquest into the death of Constable Davies, held by the coroner for East Worcestershire, Ralph Docker, at the Red Lion public house at Alvechurch. The coroner expressed his displeasure that many of the items of evidence had already be sent for analysis at the Home Office Laboratory, telling Superintendent Tyler that the inquest should have been permitted to examine things as they were found, rather than after they had been tampered with. The inquest was adjourned several times to allow the police time to carry out their investigations, although the jury eventually returned a verdict of 'guilty of wilful murder' against Moses Shrimpton and agreed that Mary Morton should be tried as an accessory after the crime.

The Red Lion public house at Alvechurch. (© N. Sly, 2008)

On 13 March, Mary Morton asked if she might see Shrimpton and was taken to his cell. As soon as she saw him, she began to cry. 'Pity the innocent should suffer for the guilty,' she told him. 'I know nothing about it and, if you will speak the truth, you know I don't. The knife you gave me on Saturday to eat my bread and cheese with, didn't you?'

'I shall say nothing,' answered Shrimpton.

Mary asked to see Moses again on 27 March and this time she asked him, 'The watch you gave me on Saturday to take to Mrs Facer, I had off you, didn't I?'

'Yes, it is my own watch. I have had it for twelve years,' replied Shrimpton.

Moses Shrimpton and Mary Morton appeared before magistrates, respectively charged with theft and wilful murder and of being an accessory to the crimes. Both pleaded 'Not Guilty', reserving their defence for their trial. Once the proceedings at the magistrate's court had concluded and the prisoners returned to gaol, a collection was taken up for the widow of Constable Davies.

The trial opened before Mr Baron Huddleston on 6 May 1885, with Mr Amphlett prosecuting, Mr Plowden defending Mary Morton and Mr Daniel acting for Moses Shrimpton.

The prosecution opened the proceedings by calling a number of witnesses who had been involved in the immediate aftermath of the discovery of the policeman's body on 28 February. These included Mr Twigg, surgeon Mr Gaunt and many of the police officers who had initiated enquiries into his death and then made the subsequent arrest of the two defendants.

One of the prosecution witnesses was Dr Shaw, who had been called to the police station to examine the wounds on Moses Shrimpton's head immediately after his arrest. Shaw stated that Shrimpton had told him that he had injured his head the previous week, falling against a lamppost while drunk. However, in Shaw's opinion, the wounds were much more recent, as they were still weeping. Shown Constable Davies' staff, Shaw agreed that it could have caused the wounds, particularly in view of the corresponding dents in Shrimpton's hat, although he also admitted that the wounds could also have occurred if Shrimpton had fallen over onto a sharp stone.

On the second day of the trial, Dr Stevenson, the Home Office Analyst, was called to the witness box. He told the court that on 7 March he had received an overcoat, a cardigan jacket and other items of clothing, a pillowcase and a double-bladed clasp knife from Superintendent Tyler, followed by a box of earth on 16 March.

He had found extensive blood staining on the overcoat, even though it had been recently washed or wiped. In fact, there had been so much blood on the sleeve that, when it dried out, he had been able to scrape it off in flakes. The trousers were muddy, particularly from the knees downwards, as if the wearer had knelt down. Mud stains on both the trousers and the coat corresponded to the samples of red soil taken from the murder scene.

There was additional blood on the flap of the right-hand trouser pocket and on the pocket lining, with yet more blood on the shirt and waistcoat. The boots were free from mud and bloodstains, save for a small droplet of blood found on the inside of one boot. The pillowcase removed from Shrimpton's room was also stained with red earth and blood, this time a mixture of mammalian and bird blood, while the blood found on the knife blade was solely mammalian.

Stevenson also gave an opinion on the wounds observed on Shrimpton's forehead on his arrest. The wounds did not appear to have bled much, which, said Stevenson, indicated that they had been more probably caused by a blunt object, rather than a fall onto a stone.

Stevenson was cross-examined by Mr Daniel, who pointed out that the soil found to have stained Shrimpton's clothes was common throughout much of Worcestershire and Warwickshire and probably even comparable to Birmingham street mud. He suggested to Stevenson that much of the mammalian blood found on Shrimpton's clothing could have come from rabbits or even from the defendant's own forehead, after he injured it. Daniel also asked Stevenson how he was able to determine the age of the bloodstains, arguing that the bloodstains could have been old ones rather than fresh.

Stevenson explained that, although he was unable to state that the blood was definitely human, he could state that it was mammalian and generally, the blood corpuscles obtained from rabbits were much smaller than those found on Shrimpton's effects. He admitted that the blood might be up to a week old, although he felt it unlikely.

The prosecution then called several more witnesses, including nine-year-old Hannah Brogden who lived at the lodging house where Shrimpton and Morton rented a room. Hannah had seen Shrimpton on the morning of 28 February and had not noticed any wounds on his forehead, although she admitted that Shrimpton kept his head down as he passed her. A little later that day, she had noticed Shrimpton's wounds and had asked Mary Morton what he had done to his head.

'Did you do it?' Hannah asked Mary, to which Mary replied, 'Yes.'

George and Mary Facer testified about receiving the watch and its subsequent destruction in the furnace at Facer's place of work.

One of the last witnesses to testify was John Whitehouse, the former landlord of the White Lion Inn at Portway, where Shrimpton was a regular drinker. Whitehouse told the court that Shrimpton appeared to have a grudge against Constable Davies and that, on one occasion he had been standing near Shrimpton when Davies had walked past the pub. 'There goes that teetotal bastard,' Shrimpton had remarked, adding, 'If ever I was to meet with him I should be a match for him.' Mrs Davies confirmed to the court that her late husband was indeed a teetotaller.

It was then left to the two defence counsels to speak for their clients. First was Mr Daniel in defence of Moses Shrimpton. Asking the jury to dismiss any prejudices they might hold against the accused, he warned them that the evidence on which they were being asked to convict him was purely circumstantial and that they should therefore give Shrimpton the benefit of any doubts that they might have.

From the word go, the police had directed all their energies into pursuing Shrimpton, said Mr Daniel, mainly because of his previous convictions for poaching and stealing poultry. He challenged the evidence given by analyst Dr Stevenson, reminding the jury that the scientist had admitted that the bloodstains could have pre-dated the policeman's murder. Daniel pointed out to the jury that the knife had a horn handle, which was naturally grooved and yet no blood had been found in the crevices in the knife handle. If, as it had been suggested, Shrimpton had stood over Constable Davies while killing him, one foot on either side of his head, then he and his clothes should have been far more liberally splattered with blood.

There was no evidence that Shrimpton was anywhere near the site of the murder and furthermore, after the officer's death, Shrimpton had not behaved like a guilty man. He had made no attempt to flee, but instead had returned home to an area where he was well known. He had not disposed of the alleged murder weapon but had used it openly in a pub to cut bread and cheese only a day after the murder. And he had made no attempt to get rid of his bloodstained clothes.

Shrimpton was sixty-six years old, an elderly man, who was rather slightly built. Constable Davies was fit, sturdy and more than thirty years his junior. Was it realistic to assume that a frail, old man could so easily overpower a much younger man?

Next came Mr Plowden in defence of Mary Morton. If it were not for the extreme gravity of the offence, said Plowden, then the charges against Mary Morton would be laughable, ludicrously disproportionate to those against Moses Shrimpton. If the jury believed Shrimpton to be guilty, did they also believe that knowledge of the crime had been brought home to his client? The prosecution would have the jury believe so, but they were working on inference, not facts, and it was unfair to ask the jury to convict Mary on inference. Her statement to the police had 'the stamp of truth from first to last,' continued Plowden and that statement had been corroborated in every substantial feature – it was a rational and probable account of what had happened. There was no legal proof of the charge against Mary Morton, he concluded, and, because of this, he believed that the jury should acquit her.

The judge then addressed the jury, telling them that if Mary Morton and Moses Shrimpton had been legally married then she could not have been charged. However, as they were unwed, she had none of the privileges of a wife and all the disadvantages. The evidence against the defendants was, admitted the judge, purely circumstantial but, at the same time, witnesses could lie but facts were facts.

This was a case of the killing of a police officer while he was discharging his duty, hence manslaughter could not apply. His duty as a policeman was to apprehend wrongdoers and if that wrongdoer resisted arrest, then Davies had every right to use violence against him. The judge called on the evidence of the footprints, suggesting that Davies had come upon Shrimpton after he had stolen the chickens and apprehended him. Shrimpton had initially gone with the officer, all the while knowing that he had the evidence of his wrongdoing still about his person in a pillowcase and in the poacher's pocket inside his coat. He had seized his opportunity to attack Davies, who had defended himself by hitting Shrimpton twice on the head with his staff. However, unbeknown to Davies, Shrimpton was armed with a knife. Davies had been stabbed and, when he had fallen to the ground, Shrimpton had finished him off by slashing his throat.

In conclusion, the judge told the jury that he could find nothing to suggest Mary Morton's complicity in the murder, apart from the fact that, as Shrimpton's mistress, she had tried to divert suspicion from him, without any knowledge of the severity of the crime with which he was charged. To this end, she had taken on the responsibility for causing his wounds. The judge then suggested that the jury should acquit Mary Morton.

The jury retired for barely five minutes before indicating to the court that they had reached a verdict. First, they pronounced Mary Morton 'Not Guilty' of the charges against her then informed the judge that they found Moses Shrimpton 'Guilty of Wilful Murder'.

Mary Morton was discharged and the judge addressed Moses Shrimpton, asking him if he had anything to say before he was sentenced.

'I am not guilty, but I am ready to die,' stated Shrimpton.

Mr Baron Huddleston then told Shrimpton that he was aware that he had a long criminal record and that he had served several prison sentences in the past. However, those crimes paled into insignificance compared with the crime for which he had just stood trial. The judge went on to sentence Shrimpton to be hanged by the neck until dead, his body afterwards buried within the prison walls.

Shrimpton met with executioner James Berry on 25 May 1885. Unfortunately, when calculating the appropriate 'drop' for Shrimpton, Berry worked solely on the man's height and failed to take into account his age and rather frail build. Thus, rather than being hung for his crime, Moses Shrimpton was decapitated; his head being ripped cleanly off his shoulders as he dropped.

Note: In contemporary newspaper accounts of the murder, George and Mary Facer are sometimes alternatively named Facey and George is sometimes referred to as William. Mary Morton's name is also frequently spelled Moreton. I have used the most common variations of all of the names in this account. Moses Shrimpton and Mary Morton apparently rented their room using the name Jackson, presumably to disguise the fact that they were unmarried. Shrimpton's age varies greatly in different contemporary newspapers, from fifty-two years old to sixty-six. The official register of deaths gives his age as sixty-six at the time of his execution.

14

'LET THE BASTARD
HAVE IT!'

Lenchwick, 1889

In the mid-nineteenth century, Wood Norton Hall, near Evesham, became home to a member of the French Royal Family when it was purchased by the Duc d'Aumale, the fourth son of Louis-Philippe, the last King of France. The magnificent house has since been owned by the BBC, who used it as a broadcasting centre during the Second World War, and is now a hotel and conference centre.

In 1889, the house was in the hands of the Duc d'Orleans, who had inherited it on the death of his great uncle two years earlier. Among the many servants he employed to run the house and estate was Frederick Stephens, who worked as a gamekeeper. Twenty-five-year-old Frederick rented a cottage in nearby Lenchwick with his wife of eighteen months and their small son.

The gamekeeper's job was a vital one on any large estate, particularly so in the Evesham area, where many of the Duc's neighbours were living in abject poverty, often struggling to bring up large families on the wages of an agricultural labourer. All too frequently, people succumbed to the temptation of poaching and, on 9 November 1889, this was the case at Wood Norton Hall.

At nine o'clock that evening, Frederick was walking the estate accompanied by fellow keeper George Baylis. They started the evening at the home of the head keeper Benjamin Wasley, at the Lenchwick crossroads. From there they did a circular tour of the estate via Hipton Hill and Craycombe Bank, before finishing back at Lenchwick at the end of their shift at two o'clock in the morning.

The two gamekeepers parted company at Lenchwick, Baylis heading back to Craycombe Bank and Stephens walking through the coppice at Lenchwick to his home. The way that he chose was not the most direct route but passed through an area that was very popular with the local poachers.

Wood Norton Hall, 1907. (Author's collection)

The entrance to Duc d'Orleans Estate, Wood Norton. (Author's collection)

Lenchwick. (© N. Sly, 2008)

It was a bright, moonlit night and Stephens had not long left his colleague when he heard a rustling noise coming from some bushes about 30 yards away. Standing stock still, he watched as three men emerged from the undergrowth, accompanied by two dogs. Each man was carrying a large bag.

Stephens waited, hidden in the shadows, until he saw one of the men taking a pot shot at a pheasant with a catapult. He then approached the men, one of whom Stephens immediately recognised as a member of the locally notorious Boswell family.

Seeing the gamekeeper approaching, Joseph Boswell shouted to his companions, 'Let the bastard have it!' at which all three of the men began to pelt the gamekeeper with stones from their pockets. However, most of the stones fell wide of their target and so Joseph decided to punch him. He swung a fist at Stephens, hitting him in the chest. Stephens crashed to the ground but managed to pull Joseph Boswell with him and a furious struggle between the two men ensued.

At one stage, Stephens had Joseph's finger in his mouth and was biting down hard on it. In agony, Joseph put his hands around the gamekeeper's throat and throttled him until he released the finger. Meanwhile, as Joseph grappled with the gamekeeper on the ground, his two companions – his brother Samuel and a friend, Alfred Hill – kicked out at Stephens, deliberately aiming their heavy boots at his head. Finally, Alfred Hill hit Stephens as hard as he could over the head with a cosh, knocking him out cold.

Frederick Stephens had been kicked and beaten almost senseless. In the course of the struggle, he had succeeded only in biting Joseph's finger and landing one blow with his stick on Samuel's head. Believing that the gamekeeper was dead, the three poachers took to their heels and fled, not wanting to be around when his body was found.

However, Stephens had not died in the attack. After about fifteen minutes, he regained consciousness and managed to half walk, half crawl the mile or so to Mr Wasley's home. Wasley answered his door at three o'clock to find Stephens on the doorstep, his face badly bruised and swollen almost beyond recognition and the top half of his body saturated with blood. Wasley immediately harnessed his horse and put Stephens in his trap, driving him at a fast pace to the Evesham surgeon, Mr Allen Haynes. Haynes examined the extensive cuts and bruising, cleaned and dressed the injuries and sent Stephens home with Mr Wasley, telling him to rest in bed.

Naturally, the police were called and, since Stephens had identified one of his attackers as Joseph Boswell to Mr Wasley, Boswell's house on Littleworth Street, Evesham, was immediately visited by Constable Brinton. As he approached the house, the policeman saw Joseph looking out of his front door. Brinton asked him what he was doing up and Joseph told him that he had been drinking earlier that night and had fallen asleep on the settee. Noticing his badly damaged finger, Brinton asked how Joseph had injured it but Joseph didn't reply. Instead, he shut the door and retreated back indoors.

The Market Place at Evesham, 1922. (Author's collection)

Brinton pushed the door, which was not on the latch and it swung open, just in time for the constable to see a figure disappearing out through the back door. 'You can come in now,' Joseph told the policeman. As Brinton stepped inside, he was rushed by a brown and white lurcher dog, which barked ferociously at him until Joseph restrained it. 'Who was that going out of the back door?' Brinton asked him.

'Nobody,' replied Joseph.

Brinton asked to see Joseph's shoes and he produced a pair that were completely dry and had obviously not been worn for some time. When Brinton asked to see any other pairs of shoes he had, Joseph exploded into a rage, telling Brinton that he had no search warrant and that he wasn't going to let him search the house. The noise of his furious outburst woke his wife, who immediately came downstairs to see what was happening. Joseph told her that if the policeman didn't leave, he intended to knock his bloody head off, at which Brinton decided that it was in his best interests to withdraw. Meanwhile, the commotion had woken the Boswell's next-door neighbour, Joseph Beard, who immediately looked out of his back window to see what all the noise was about. In Boswell's back garden, he saw Samuel Boswell and his wife, along with Alfred Hill, who all eventually scrambled over the garden wall and disappeared into the night.

On the following morning, Joseph Boswell went to visit his younger brother, James. As James was still in bed when he arrived, Joseph began chatting to his brother's wife, Elizabeth. 'Don't split,' he told her, 'but we have bloody nigh killed the keeper.' He related the events of the previous night in great detail, even down to imitating the choking noises Stephens had made when Joseph was throttling him. Joseph also told Elizabeth about the policeman coming to his door, saying that his brother Sam and Albert Hill had been hiding upstairs at the time and had eventually escaped through his back garden.

Elizabeth kept the secret for about a week, until it became known that Frederick Stephens' condition was worsening. His employers had paid for a nurse to attend him throughout his illness and, when it became apparent that he was fading, they called in Mr Haynes, who decided that the young man was suffering from compression of the brain and operated on him. Once Frederick was under the knife, Haynes found a small piece of broken skull, which was exerting pressure on the surface of his brain. Haynes removed the loose piece of bone, but Stephens made no improvement.

The Duc agreed to pay for specialist treatment for his employee, so Haynes called in two eminent surgeons, Dr Bennett May and Dr Strange, who performed a second operation, this time removing a much larger section of his skull. Initially, Stephens seemed to rally after his second surgery, but he soon began to suffer from convulsions and eventually lapsed into a coma. He had just one more short period of full consciousness, before dying on 23 November 1889.

It was only at the post-mortem examination that the full extent of his injuries was realised. Haynes found that Frederick Stephens had two massive fractures in his skull, the largest being 5in in length. The damage to Stephens' skull was consistent with him either having been hit with a blunt instrument or kicked and Haynes expressed surprise that such major injuries could have initially produced such minor symptoms.

By the time Stephens died, the police had already arrested Joseph and Samuel Boswell and, because they knew that three men had been involved, much to his displeasure, another brother, James, was also arrested. All three men were taken before magistrates, charged with trespassing for the purpose of night poaching and additionally, in the case of Joseph and Samuel, with unlawfully wounding and inflicting grievous bodily harm with intent on Frederick Stephens. Joseph and Samuel attended the proceedings in their working clothes, but James, who was outraged at being implicated, arrived in his Sunday best suit.

Before his death, Stephens was well enough to give a deposition, in which he described seeing three men approaching through the woods with their two dogs, one of which was a lurcher and the other a white or light-coloured dog of indeterminate breed. Stephens stated that one of the men had definitely been Joseph Boswell.

Joseph Boswell was brought to Stephen's bedside, along with his older brother, Samuel, and his younger brother, James, who was known to own a lurcher dog. Stephens positively identified Joseph as one of his assailants, saying when challenged by him, 'I will be on my dying oath that you are one of the men. You worked for Mr Randall about three years ago.' He did not identify James as one of his attackers and was unsure about Samuel. He first said that Samuel had been present, but Samuel and Joseph looked very alike and Stephens just couldn't be absolutely sure.

Stephens went on to describe the stones that had been thrown at him and the fight with Joseph Boswell, during which the other two men kicked him as he struggled on the ground. He recalled being hit with a stick, but could only remember taking a blow to his shoulders. He described the bags the men had been carrying as 'like guano bags', saying that they appeared to be about three-quarters full and that the men had taken the bags away with them when they left him unconscious. When Wasley and George Baylis examined the scene of the attack with the police, they found that all the physical evidence corroborated Stephen's statement. There were obvious signs of a scuffle having taken place and an outline of a man's body in blood on the ground. The area was scattered with stones and five pegs were found, of the kind used to hold nets for catching rabbits and other game. One of the pegs, which was about 30in long, bore traces of human hair, similar in appearance to the hair from Frederick Stephens's whiskers. A man's blue handkerchief was also found in the wood, near to where the attack had taken place.

Stephens' deposition was read in the magistrate's court and an application was made to remand all three men in custody pending further investigations by the police. Both Joseph and Samuel swore that they had been elsewhere on the night of the attack on the gamekeeper, saying that they could produce witnesses to prove it. Joseph also said that, contrary to Stephens' assertions, he had never worked for Mr Randall in his life.

Joseph asked for bail, saying that he had a wife and young children, but his request was turned down. James, on the other hand, was granted bail but immediately began to argue that the amount set was too high. He began a furious rant against the magistrates, sobbing and shouting, 'I b'ain't going to be locked up,' and demanding compensation for his lost time. He was eventually forcibly removed from the court to cool down and, when he was brought back, the magistrates had discussed his situation between themselves and the offer of bail was withdrawn.

Once Frederick Stephens died, Joseph and Samuel Boswell were immediately charged with his wilful murder. They appeared before magistrates again for the elevated charge, along with James, who was still facing the original charge of trespassing for the purpose of poaching.

In an unexpected twist, James was formally discharged and immediately afterwards, his wife Elizabeth testified about the conversation she had had with Joseph on the morning after the murder, implicating Alfred Hill as the third assailant. She identified the blue handkerchief found at the scene of the murder as belonging to Alfred Hill, telling the court that, when Hill's wife had been seriously ill, she had taken in the family's washing to help them out and had personally washed the handkerchief numerous times. Elizabeth also admitted that her husband owned a lurcher dog but said that it was kept in an easily accessible outhouse and would quite happily go off with either Joseph or Samuel.

Once she had given her evidence, Joseph and Samuel Boswell were invited to speak. Samuel continued to maintain his innocence, saying that he had been playing cards at the Jolly Gardener public house at the time of the murder, while Joseph simply accused his sister-in-law of making up stories against him. He then told the magistrates, 'you have not got the man what gave him the smack what coopered him sir, if he is dead, sir.'

The magistrates asked him if, by that, he meant that they did not have the man who struck the fatal blow.

'No, sir. There was but one blow struck and that was all, sir.'

Samuel and Joseph were remanded for a further week and the police issued a description of Alfred Hill, who seemed to have fled the area. Hill, who was nicknamed 'Lovely', was twenty-three years old and stood about 5ft 6ins tall, He had a round, full face and high cheekbones with a fresh complexion, light hair and hazel eyes, with a light moustache. He had several tattoos and scars, including two boil marks on his lower back. He was bow-legged and had thick strong fingers. A native of Evesham, he had previously been employed as a market gardener but could also turn his hand to farm labouring and working with horses.

When last seen, he was wearing a grey jacket, dark cord trousers, boots and a soft, black billycock hat. He often walked with his hands in his pockets and was known for using coarse language and, when drunk, would often sing the song 'Don't put my father's picture up for sale'.

Alfred came from a respectable family and was the youngest of ten children. Yet he had had frequent brushes with the law, starting with an arrest, aged thirteen, for stealing toys from a shop. He had seen Joseph being arrested through the window of the Trumpet Inn and had immediately begun boasting to the other patrons that the police had got the wrong man. When the police later arrived to arrest him, his friends helped him by boosting him over a wall into fields at the back of the pub.

Hill walked through the fields to his home where he asked his wife for some money, saying that he was intending to bail James Boswell. Instead, he took the money and fled to his brother's house in Birmingham. There he found himself a job as a coke runner at the Gas Works in Windsor Street, going by the name of George Hale and living in a rented room in Dartmouth Street. A tip-off to the police led to his eventual arrest.

Joseph and Samuel Boswell and Alfred Hill were tried for the murder before Mr Justice Hawkins, and, as at the magistrate's court, the trial involved much bickering and squabbling among the various members of the Boswell family. However, the witness who perhaps made the biggest impression on the jury was a labourer named Thomas Spragg, who had been drinking in the Jolly Gardener Inn on the evening of the murder.

Spragg told the court that Joseph had been in the pub and that Samuel had come in to fetch him and asked him if he was ready. Spragg swore that he had heard the men saying, 'Let any bastard come and we will knock his bloody head off!' This tied in with the remark 'Let the bastard have it!' that Stephens had mentioned in his deposition and also with Joseph threatening to knock Constable Brinton's 'bloody head off' and, in the minds of the jury, seemed to indisputably connect the defendants with the murder.

Still, the jury debated for three hours before returning with their verdict, apparently because one of their number could not agree with the views of the remaining jurors. He eventually capitulated and all three men were found guilty and sentenced to death.

A petition of more than 2,000 signatures was sent to the Home Secretary asking for a reprieve for the three prisoners. The petition cast doubts on the behaviour of the foreman of the jury and on Spragg's evidence, which all of the condemned men maintained was untrue. Additionally, there had been only one fatal blow and it was not possible to ascertain which of the three men had struck it. Finally, the petitioners pointed out that, if the executions went ahead, no less than ten young children would be rendered fatherless.

Meanwhile, all three men were preparing for death at Worcester Prison. All three wrote to their wives, the Boswells dictating their letters and Alfred Hill penning his own letter in a childish hand:

If so be that God spare my life to see the wide world once more you will find me a different husband, for this as learned me your word which you used to say 'I would not go out tonight.' I think of it many times in a day: that don't make it no better. I will trust to the Lord Almighty to see me through my troubles. [*sic*]

On 8 March, the families of all three of the condemned men went to the prison to say their last goodbyes. James Berry, the executioner, arrived at Worcester and began to prepare for the hanging. However, on the day before the scheduled executions, a surprise memorandum arrived from the Home Secretary – one of the three prisoners was to be reprieved.

Thus, it was only Joseph and Samuel Boswell who walked to the scaffold on 10 March 1890. Alfred Hill – the person who the Boswells had maintained throughout had struck the fatal blow – had his sentence commuted to one of life imprisonment.

As the two men neared the gallows, Samuel's nerve deserted him and he sagged at the knees in a swoon. He was eventually lifted onto the scaffold. White hoods were placed over the heads of both men, at which Joseph suddenly cried out, 'Lord have mercy on us.'

'Christ have mercy on us,' responded Samuel.

'Oh, my poor dear wife and my poor dear children,' lamented Joseph. The two men then bade each other 'Goodbye', Samuel adding, 'God bless you, my boy.'

'I hope everything will be all right,' said Joseph, at which the traps fell, leaving the Boswells suspended by their necks in mid-air.

The poaching trip on 9 November 1889 had netted just four rabbits in total but had ultimately cost the lives of three men, not to mention the ruination of the life of a fourth, Alfred Hill. The deaths of the poachers left nine children fatherless and the Parish Guardians at Evesham subsequently ruled that their wives were to get no financial assistance in raising them. Of course, the murder of Frederick Stephens left his son fatherless too, although the boy was generously provided for by the Duc d'Orleans.

Note: Alfred Hill seemed to have been most commonly known by his nickname, which is variously given in contemporary accounts of the case as 'Lovely' and 'Lively'.

15

'LIFE IS WORTH LITTLE TO ME'

Long Eye, 1893

The dapper young man walked the streets around Bromsgrove, knocking on doors. Whenever anybody answered, he smiled politely and held up a card, which read: 'Pardon me for asking you to buy. I am deaf and dumb.' Then, if the occupant of the house didn't immediately shoo him away, he would open the box he carried, which contained paper, envelopes and other small items such as collar studs. He had a neatly trimmed black moustache and large, dark, intelligent eyes and was respectably dressed, almost seeming to exude an air of refinement. Sometimes people bought something from him and sometimes they sent him on his way. Others took pity on him and gave him a penny or two without buying.

By 9 January 1893, the travelling hawker had reached Long Eye, near Lickey End. There, Joseph Pearcey and his wife, Charlotte, kept a small shop in the front room of their cottage, which they ran in tandem with a small depot supplying coal from an adjoining yard. Joseph was sixty-nine years old and his wife two years older and the couple had no children. Their small businesses helped them to live reasonably comfortably in their old age.

The hawker called into the shop in the morning and held up his card for Joseph to read. Joseph, who described himself as 'no scholar', was unable to read all the words but gathered that the man wanted him to buy some of the paper that he was carrying. Joseph looked at the man's samples but politely declined to buy anything from him. The man gestured that he wished to make a purchase from the shop and eventually walked away with a halfpenny bag of apples.

Joseph thought no more about him until the following Friday, which was 13 January. That morning Joseph woke up feeling unwell and Charlotte told him to stay in bed, promising to call the doctor to attend to him. Joseph lay dozing in bed, waking up with a start when he heard footsteps coming up the stairs and saw a man walking into his bedroom. At first he wasn't unduly worried, thinking that it was the doctor's assistant. The man had his back to Joseph, who suddenly realised that the stranger was rummaging through some boxes at the end of his bed, turning the contents out onto the floor.

Joseph began to get out of bed, intending to challenge the man but, as soon as he moved, the man turned to look at him, before bolting out of the bedroom. Recognising the intruder as the deaf and dumb peddler, Joseph gave chase but, as he went downstairs, he heard the front door slamming shut and by the time Joseph reached the shop the man had gone.

Worryingly for Joseph, there was no sign of Charlotte. He called out to her, asking where she was but there was no reply. Joseph began to look for her and, as he walked behind the shop counter, he found her.

Charlotte Pearcey was lying unconscious on the floor, blood pouring from a wound in her head and an orange tightly clutched in one hand. Joseph ran to the shop door to raise the alarm, but found the door locked against him. He rushed to get a spanner and a chisel and eventually smashed the lock and ran out into the road.

The Pearcey's house was in an isolated rural area, some 50 yards from the house of their nearest neighbour, a single woman named Mabel Sanders. Pearcey's desperate shouts eventually attracted Mabel's attention and she ran to see what the matter was. Another neighbour, Ellen Noakes, had been at the yard earlier that morning buying coal. She had paid Charlotte Pearcey and then loaded up a wheelbarrow with coal, pushing it to her house, about 120 yards away. She emptied the barrow, returned to the coal yard and refilled it, pushing the second load home and emptying it into her coal shed before setting out again to return the wheelbarrow. As she was leaving the yard for the third time, Ellen heard banging sounds from inside the house as Joseph Pearcey struggled to smash the lock. Moments later, he burst out of the shop and began to shout for help.

Mabel went into the house to see what she could do to help Charlotte, accompanied by a farmer, Thomas Weaver, who just happened to be walking by. Ellen and Jane Adams, another passer-by, hurried to summon the police and a doctor. Dr Richard Wood arrived just before midday but there was absolutely nothing that he could do; Charlotte had suffered a massive wound to the top of her head, inflicted with sufficient violence to cause her blood and brain tissue to be liberally splattered around the shop. She died at about four o'clock that afternoon, without ever having regained consciousness.

Constable Clarke arrived at the Pearcey's shop, followed shortly afterwards by Sergeant Howard and Superintendent Jeffrey. They first asked Pearcey if Charlotte's attacker had stolen anything but the old man wasn't sure. He told the police that there was usually some money in the shop and that it was kept in a can. The can was now empty, although Joseph could not be absolutely certain that it had contained any money that morning. When he went upstairs to check his bedroom, he found an axe that did not belong to him hidden in a trunk. The axe handle was stamped with the name H. Daly and the blade was covered with fresh blood, to which a single grey hair adhered. Pearcey gave the axe, which was obviously the murder weapon, to Superintendent Jeffrey.

The police began immediate enquiries at the few houses near to the little shop and found a number of people who purported to have seen a tramp hanging around the area over the past few days. They described him as a well-built man, under thirty years old, who carried with him a sign stating that he was deaf and dumb and a box of wares.

The police soon managed to locate the H. Daly, whose name was stamped on the murder weapon. Henry Daly was a joiner who told them that, on 12 January, he had been working at a shop in Great Colmore Street, Birmingham. That afternoon, a man had stood nearby, watching Daly and his gang working for almost an hour. At about four o'clock, Daly had gone out to the back of the shop to burn some waste material, putting the axe down on the window sill, close to where the man was standing. Wanting to chop some wood to fuel his fire, Daly came back a little later to collect the axe but it had vanished and so had the watching man. Daly's colleague, Edward Poynton, confirmed his story.

Having located the owner of the axe, the police now began to question people who lived close to the shop where he had been working. Soon, they came across a woman whose lodger had recently disappeared under mysterious circumstances.

Rachel Levi and her husband, Samuel, let a few rooms at their home in Great Colmore Street and, in November 1892, a Mr Pendare and his wife had taken one of those rooms. Pendare went out every day with a box of stationery for sale and, according to Mrs Levi, he was not deaf and dumb, but a foreigner. On 13 January, he left her house at nine o'clock in the morning and returned between two and three o'clock that afternoon, going straight to his room. He did not come out of his room again until the following Tuesday, when a cab arrived to collect him at just after five o'clock and he left, carrying a large box. Mrs Levi had not seen him since but told the police that Mrs Pendare was still living at her house.

Mrs Pendare was interviewed and admitted that the name Pendare was a pseudonym. Mr Pendare was actually a Frenchman named Amie Holman Meunier and he had left her on 17 January, telling her that the police were after him for stealing items belonging to Captain Davy, for whom he had formerly worked as a valet. On the day of the murder, her husband had come home in the afternoon looking pale and ill and had burned the clothes he had been wearing that day. When he left, he had told her that he was heading for the continent to escape the police and that he would contact her shortly.

The police contacted their European counterparts with a description of Meunier, who was very quickly arrested in Brussels, Belgium. Extradition proceedings were started, to allow Meunier to be brought back to England, and eventually Octave Reny, a sergeant in the Belgian Mounted Constabulary, escorted Meunier from Brussels to Ostend and from there across the Channel to Dover, aboard the steamship *Prince*.

At Dover, at two o'clock in the morning of 14 February 1893, Meunier was formally handed over to Constable Clarke and Superintendent Wasley from the Worcestershire Constabulary.

During his journey with the police officer from Belgium, Meunier had made what amounted to a full confession to the murder of Charlotte Pearcey. It had been in French, his native language, and Reny was able to provide the constables from Worcestershire with an English translation.

'I know I am going to be hanged in England for the murder I committed at Bromsgrove,' said Meunier to his escort. 'Life is worth little to me. I have killed and I must pay the debt.' Meunier then went on to to tell Reny an extraordinary tale about being a member of an organisation called The Anarchists in Birmingham. According to Meunier, a member of the organisation had been convicted of an offence by a magistrate in Bromsgrove and the group had subsequently met and decided to get revenge on the magistrate by killing him. Meunier had been elected to do the deed.

He had broken into what he believed to be the magistrate's house and found the old woman in his way, so had killed her. However, he had baulked at killing Joseph too and had fled back to Birmingham. Meunier expressed great sadness at causing suffering to his wife and promised that, if the magistrates didn't deal with him too severely, he might 'reveal certain facts to English justice.'

Once in the custody of the Worcestershire Police, Meunier had made several statements, despite having told them, 'Me not understand much English.' When he was asked directly about the murder he replied, 'Me not say no, me say yes, it was me. Me very sorry.'

New Road, Bromsgrove, 1905. (Author's collection)

Twenty-five-year-old Meunier was charged with the wilful murder of Charlotte Pearcey and committed for trial at the Worcester Assizes. His trial opened before Mr Baron Pollock on 28 June 1893. The case had already progressed through the normal route of magistrate's court appearances, at which Meunier had openly declared his guilt and pronounced himself ready and willing to meet his fate. He had declined all offers to provide a defence counsel to act on his behalf. However, at the beginning of June, he had suddenly changed his mind and decided that he would like to be defended after all. Meunier's friends raised sufficient money to pay for this and Mr Marchant had been instructed. He was opposed in court by Mr A.R. Jelf QC and Mr Reginald Smith, who conducted the prosecution.

Mr Jelf opened the proceedings by calling a number of witnesses who had all seen Meunier in the Bromsgrove area in the days immediately prior to the murder. These included Joseph Pearcey and those people who had rushed to his aid, as well as several local people who had been approached to buy paper by the 'deaf and dumb' peddler. All of these witnesses had picked Meunier out at an identity parade, as had Henry Daly and his workmate. Witnesses who lived near Meunier in Birmingham were also called to testify and the booking clerk at Bromsgrove station, Thomas Patrick, told the court that he had sold Meunier a railway ticket on the afternoon of the murder. Meunier had initially wanted to go from Bromsgrove to Birmingham, but had missed the train, settling instead for travelling to Droitwich. Patrick too had picked Meunier out at an identification parade.

Rachel Levi told the court about her lodger, whom she knew only as Mr Pendare, and was cross-examined extensively by Mr Marchant about the man's strange behaviour. Marchant pressed her to say that, at times, she had said that she thought her lodger had 'gone off his head'. Mrs Levi would only concede that Meunier had behaved very strangely on a couple of occasions and, at those times, she might have thought him a little odd but had taken very little notice because he was 'foreign'.

Octave Reny had travelled from Brussels to appear in court and related Meunier's confession, made while he was under escort to England. Marchant cross-examined him, paying particular attention to the references to the society of anarchists that the defendant had mentioned. There was, said Marchant, a notorious anarchist named Meunier active in Paris at the time. Did the defendant believe that he was that Meunier, asked Marchant? Reny admitted that he had not questioned the defendant, so didn't know what he believed. However, Reny knew that the defendant wasn't the Paris Meunier, as he had seen photographs of him. During his defence counsel's interrogation of Reny on the subject of anarchists, Meunier laughed out loud.

The next witness to be called was Dr Cooke, the medical superintendent of the Powick Asylum, who had been requested by the Treasury to investigate Meunier's mental health. He told the court that he had examined the defendant on a number of occasions in May and June. Cooke had also received reports from the prison warders in charge of Meunier, which stated that his behaviour in custody had been 'troublesome'. He alternately cried and laughed inappropriately and had also sung and danced while in his cell. He had a habit of continually nodding his head, sometimes for periods of more than six hours and he frequently banged his head against his pillow or the wall of his cell.

On 23 March he had made an attempt at suicide, which was thwarted by his vigilant warders. Cooke told the court that, while he was not of the opinion that Meunier was of unsound mind, there was a definite period immediately following his suicide attempt when his mind was 'unhinged'.

Marchant asked Cooke if Meunier's mind might also have been unhinged in January 1893, to which Cooke replied that it was possible but that, having considered all the evidence, he believed it was unlikely.

Cooke then went on to discuss Meunier's medical history. Meunier had suffered a serious head injury in the past when he had been struck by a falling girder. Cooke said that such a blow on the head might conceivably lead to insanity, but this blow had happened a considerable time prior to the murder and he did not believe that it had adversely affected Meunier's mental state. Cooke had spoken to Meunier's mother and had learned that his father had died in a fit of drunkenness soon after his birth. Cooke said that it was often the case that the children of drunken parents were 'more or less affected in the head' but, other than that, he had found no history of any nervous diseases in Meunier's family. Meunier himself had been treated in several hospitals in France, but Cooke could not establish whether or not this was for insanity. He was therefore of the opinion that Meunier was not insane at the time of the murder.

Cooke's testimony must have come as something of a blow to Mr Marchant, whose entire defence was based on Meunier's insanity. Nevertheless, he pressed on with his summary, reminding the jury that his client's father had died from acute intoxication and that Meunier had also received a head injury that had been sufficiently severe to merit hospital treatment in France. Marchant reminded the jury of incidences of 'strangeness' that the defendant had exhibited while lodging with Mrs Levi, saying that nobody had any idea how many times in the past Meunier had experienced 'fits of fury'.

Marchant dismissed the idea that the motive for Mrs Pearcey's murder had been robbery, saying instead that it was a purposeless crime, committed while the defendant was insane and that the ingenuity that Meunier had displayed in initially evading capture may well have been the kind of ingenuity often associated with madness. There was evidence that Meunier had now recovered from his temporary insanity but the jury should find that he was insane at the time of the murder, in which case he would be detained in an asylum for the rest of his natural life.

Mr Baron Pollock then summed up the case for the jury. He began by congratulating both counsels for the way in which they had handled the case according to the best traditions of British justice, something he felt especially important since the defendant was a foreigner. He then went on to address the issues surrounding the insanity defence, telling the jury that it was not a question of whether the prisoner had suffered an aberration of mind either before or after the murder. It was for the jury to decide whether the accused was of unsound mind at the time at which the crime was committed.

The jury retired very briefly before returning with a verdict of 'Guilty of Wilful Murder' against Amie Meunier, who showed no reaction as his interpreter translated the verdict for him. When asked by the judge if he had anything to say after sentence of death had been pronounced, Meunier thanked the judge for his sentence but declined to make any further comment, leaving the dock with a gesture to the spectators, poking his finger into his neck and laughing.

Meunier tried again to commit suicide in the condemned cell at Worcester Prison but ultimately survived to meet executioner James Billington on 19 July 1893.

16

'TELL WILL HIS MOTHER'S NEARLY DEAD'

Foxlydiate, 1902

On 10 May 1902, Mrs Harriet Hassall of Foxlydiate near Redditch was awakened at midnight by the sound of a quarrel between Samuel Middleton and his wife Hannah, who lived in the cottage adjoining hers. The argument appeared to be about Hannah's refusal to hand over the proceeds of the sale of some potatoes to her husband and Mrs Hassall immediately resigned herself to a very disturbed night.

Samuel was a forty-five-year-old general labourer who, when sober, was a pleasant, easy-going man. However, he indulged in frequent bouts of heavy drinking and Mrs Hassall knew that, in drink, Samuel was 'a very terror' to his long-suffering wife. Hannah, who was about five years older than her husband, was clean and sober, a good woman and a good neighbour, who always did her best for her home and husband, as well as at her work as a charwoman in the neighbourhood. Yet whenever Samuel had been drinking, she often spent all night walking the lanes, too afraid of him to go home.

Mrs Hassall's bedroom was separated from that of her neighbours only by a thin wall. The quarrel between the Middleton's continued noisily for an hour, and then at one o'clock in the morning, she heard a sudden short scream, followed by an outpouring of swear words. After that, there was no more shouting, although somebody next door was still moving around and ran up and down the stairs several times, as well as going in and out of the cottage more than once. Finally, the noises ceased and the exhausted Mrs Hassall immediately fell asleep.

She awoke two hours later to find her bedroom full of smoke and realised that her house was on fire. Being elderly and quite infirm, as well as being almost paralysed by fear, it took her several minutes to get up and throw on enough clothes to preserve her modesty. She then went outside as fast as she could and banged on the door of Thomas and Laura Drew, who lived opposite her.

The Redditch fire brigade were summoned at half-past four in the morning and were at the scene within thirty minutes. They found that the Middleton's home was the source of the fire and was by then a blazing inferno, with the flames rapidly spreading to Mrs Hassall's home. While the fire brigade fought desperately to douse the flames at the Middleton's home, neighbours rushed in and out of Mrs Hassall's cottage and managed to save some of her smaller possessions. However, it was soon evident that the firemen were fighting a losing battle and at six o'clock in the morning, the roof and upper floors of the Middleton's home collapsed. Shortly afterwards, Mrs Hassall's roof also fell in and it was almost seven o'clock in the morning before the fire was under control. By then, all that remained of the Middleton's cottage were the blackened outer walls and the chimney.

The firemen began a careful search of the debris and, at just before eight o'clock, the charred remains of a woman were found on the floor of the kitchen. The head, arms and legs had burned almost entirely away, leaving a torso that resembled a burnt log of wood. Beneath the body were a few remnants of a woman's brown dress with buttons up the back.

In the midst of the conflagration, the Middleton's son, William, had arrived home in a state of panic. He told the fire brigade that, at three o'clock in the morning, his father had called at his place of work and banged on the door of Joseph Worskett, the gamekeeper for his employer, Lord Windsor. When Worskett came to his bedroom window to see who wanted him, Middleton shouted a message to him.

'Tell Will his mother's nearly dead.'

Before Worskett could ask any questions, Middleton turned on his heel and disappeared into the night.

His next port of call was at the home of his eighty-four-year-old mother at Upper Bentley. He called up to her window, 'Goodbye, Mother. Annie's dead by this time. Will you go?' and then walked off without waiting to hear her reply.

At six o'clock the next morning, salt maker James Workman was returning from a nightshift when he noticed a man lying face down in the road at Wychbold, between Bromsgrove and Droitwich. The man didn't appear to be breathing and, when Workman touched him, he found that he was stone cold. He was about fifty years old and, from his clothing, was apparently a respectable working man, although his face, hands and chest were mysteriously blackened.

Workman summoned the police. Constable Hayes arrived and, having searched the dead man's pockets, could find nothing that might provide any clues to his identity. He reported the discovery of the corpse back to his superior officer, Superintendent Jeffrey of Droitwich, who was aware that his Redditch colleagues were searching for Samuel Middleton and believed that he might possibly have found him. Jeffrey contacted Inspector Hayes who immediately collected William Middleton and drove him in his trap to view the body. However, William could not be sure whether the body was that of his father – he thought it was, but just couldn't say with absolute certainty.

Hayes drove him back to Foxlydiate and picked up the Middleton's neighbour, Thomas Drew, along with Herbert Chambers, the landlord of the local pub, the Fox and Goose, both of whom had known Middleton well. When the two men viewed the body, they were far more positive about the man's identity – he was not Samuel Middleton.

A later post-mortem examination of the dead man showed that, whoever he was, he was absolutely riddled with disease and did not appear to have eaten for some time, surviving only on a mixture of beer and stimulants. He had died from a combination of exposure and malnutrition.

Since Samuel Middleton had not been seen after leaving his mother's home in the early hours of the morning of the fire, the police were leaning towards the idea that he had taken his own life and accordingly Inspector Hayes made arrangements for local lakes and pools to be dragged and drained. However, before his orders could be carried out, Middleton was spotted wandering aimlessly down a country lane near Worcester, around 14 miles from his home. Constable Bird was sent to investigate the sighting and approached the man, asking him if his name was Samuel Middleton. 'I suppose it must be,' the man replied. Bird took him to Droitwich police station, where he was judged to be under the influence of drink and thus not fit to be questioned. Superintendent Jeffrey telegraphed his Redditch colleagues to tell them that he had Middleton in custody and, after spending a night in the cells to sober up, Middleton was transported to Redditch police station, where he was charged both with the wilful murder of his wife and with arson.

He showed no reaction to the charges against him and still seemed dazed and confused when he was taken to Worcester Prison, where he was to await the commencement of legal proceedings against him.

An inquest into the death of Hannah Middleton was opened before Mr Ralph Docker, the coroner for East Worcestershire, at which Samuel declined to be present. Laura Drew gave evidence of identification, having identified her neighbour only by the scraps of clothes found under the body and then told the inquest of a visit she had made to the Middleton's cottage on the afternoon of the fire. Samuel and Hannah had already started arguing and Samuel had tipped over the kitchen table, having first thrown his supper at the wall. 'Look what my husband has done,' Hannah said to Laura.

When Laura Drew called at the Middleton's home, Samuel was angrily demanding money from his wife, who was refusing to give it to him. About half an hour after Laura returned home, Hannah appeared on her doorstep and furtively gave Laura her purse, telling her, 'If anything happens to me, give this to my boy.'

Hannah then went to Herbert Chambers at the Fox and Goose to ask him to come and talk to her husband. When Chambers arrived, he found Samuel in 'an excited state', although he did not appear to be drunk. There was smashed crockery scattered about the Middleton's kitchen and Chambers warned Samuel about controlling his temper. Samuel was obviously not pleased about the pub landlord's attempts at mediation between him and his wife and threatened Chambers with violence.

After Herbert Chambers had left, Hannah again went to Laura Drew and asked her to come home with her. Mrs Drew did so and stayed at the Middleton's house until ten past eleven that evening, by which time Samuel had apparently calmed down and the couple seemed to be on good terms again. Of course, Mrs Hassall was later to tell the inquest that the argument had flared up again and had woken her at midnight.

William Middleton stated that he had frequently heard his father threatening his mother, especially in the past two or three months. Samuel Middleton's elderly mother, Ann, was brought to the inquest accompanied by a hospital nurse and tried her hardest to give evidence but she was so distressed and ill that she was completely unable to speak and was eventually escorted from the room without having testified.

The various police officers and firemen who had attended the fire spoke of finding the remains of Hannah Middleton in the debris. Constable Lyes stated that a broken poker and a pair of fire tongs had been found less than 2ft away from the body, while an axe head weighing 5–6lbs had been found in the next room. A billhook and the broken end of the poker lay next to it. In addition, there had been a trail of fresh straw leading from the pigsty outside to the house.

Constable Broome, who had been in charge of Samuel Middleton when he was first taken into custody, told the coroner that Middleton had made a statement. 'It is very aggravating but it can't be helped now,' said Middleton. 'I dressed myself and tried to get out of the house but her clung to me and I had to finish her. I was not going to be set on by a woman.' He pointed to a scratch on his cheek and told the policeman, 'My woman done this' [sic], later admitting that he had hit her on the head with a poker because she wouldn't let go of him and kept following him around.

The next witness to appear was James Tyler, a roadman, who had reported seeing Middleton wandering about the lanes to the police. Tyler related a strange conversation that he had had with Middleton, who had approached him while he was working on the roads and asked, 'Where am I going?'

'Where do you want to go?' replied Tyler.

'Anywhere. Anywhere. I have killed my wife. They will soon catch me,' said Middleton, before walking off again.

The final witness at the inquest was Dr Matthews, who had performed a post-mortem examination on Hannah's remains. Her body had been so thoroughly consumed by the fire that Matthews was unable to find any evidence of signs of violence towards her and was also unable to say whether she had already been dead when the fire started or if she had perished in the flames.

Having heard all the evidence, the coroner's jury returned a verdict of wilful murder against Samuel Middleton and at a subsequent appearance before magistrates he was committed for trial at the next Worcester Assizes. Pitifully, his mother tried to give evidence at the magistrate's court but, once again, was unable to speak. At the magistrate's request, she was examined by Dr Matthews, who was in court to give his own testimony. Matthews felt that the old woman would be able to testify if she could be allowed to do so without the stress of being in court. Arrangements were quickly made to take a deposition from her, in which she spoke of her son's brief visit to her home in the early hours of the morning of the fire.

Middleton's trial opened before Mr Justice Wright on 25 June 1902. Mr Amphlett KC and Mr Farrant appeared for the prosecution, while Mr Carmichael conducted Middleton's defence. Middleton himself appeared totally confused by the proceedings and spent most of his time gazing blankly out of a window.

He showed no emotion whatsoever as all the witnesses who had testified in his absence at the inquest gave their personal accounts of the death of his wife. Even the pathetic appearance of his mother in the witness box did not move him, although the old lady was terribly frail and sobbed bitterly as she struggled to give her testimony.

After all the witnesses had been heard, Middleton remained detached and apparently disinterested as Mr Carmichael rose to begin his defence. Carmichael told the jury that he was not going to suggest to them that his client did not cause the death of his wife, but that at the time Samuel had been so much under the influence of drink that he had been totally incapable of forming any intention to kill her. He conceded that Middleton had made several damning statements to numerous people about his actions on the night of the tragedy, but proposed that Middleton had been so drunk that the reliability of these statements was called into question.

Furthermore, all of the witness statements led to the belief that there had been a degree of provocation on Hannah's part. Mrs Hassall had testified to hearing two voices arguing on the night of the fire and, when he had asked her if Hannah usually gave as good as she got in the couple's frequent quarrels, Mrs Hasall had agreed that she did, saying, 'Women have generally got a bit to say.'

The police had testified that Samuel Middleton had a scratch on his nose at the time of his arrest. Carmichael told the jury that he believed that Hannah and Samuel had struggled when he had tried to leave the house and she had attempted to prevent him from leaving. In the scuffle, a lamp or a candle had been accidentally overturned, starting the fire. It was, said Carmichael, a case of manslaughter at worst.

Mr Justice Wright summed up the case for the jury, instructing them on what would be considered sufficient provocation to reduce the charge from one of wilful murder to manslaughter. A mere scratch from a woman was not enough. The jury would need to find evidence of considerable provocation such as an insult or a

Mr Justice Wright. (Author's collection)

blow, to which the accused immediately retaliated with the intention of punishing rather than killing. Hannah merely trying to prevent her husband from leaving the house did not excuse the violence towards her and neither did drunkenness, if indeed the accused was drunk at the time. Warning the jury to be cautious about relying solely on Middleton's various statements he told them that, in order to reach their verdict, they must first determine the likelihood of Hannah having offered any violence towards her husband immediately before her death.

The jury deliberated for ten minutes before returning with a verdict of 'Guilty of Wilful Murder' against Samuel Middleton, who continued to show no reaction whatsoever on hearing the verdict and the pronunciation of the death sentence upon him. Other than pleading 'Not Guilty' at the start of the trial, he had taken no interest in what was happening around him, sitting calmly stroking his beard as if in a dream. Having sentenced Middleton to death, the judge then formally dismissed the charge of arson against him.

On 15 July 1902, Samuel Middleton mounted the scaffold still in an almost trance-like state, to be quickly despatched by William Billington. His body was later buried within the prison walls.

Note: Hannah Middleton is frequently referred to as Annie Middleton in contemporary accounts of the murder. It seems likely that she was usually known as Annie. There are some discrepancies between the reports of the case in different newspapers – for example the descriptions of the condition of Annie's remains vary considerably and there are also different occupations given for the defendant and some of the witnesses. There are also references to both a Constable and an Inspector Hayes – it is assumed that these are two different police officers with the same name but different rank.

17

'MURDER WILL OUT SOME DAY'

On 4 October 1903, herdsman Fred Perry was driving his cows from their field to Aggborough Farm, Kidderminster, for morning milking, when the leading cow suddenly stopped dead, flatly refusing to go any further. When Fred went to see what had spooked her, he could just make out the body of a woman lying on the lane.

Somehow he managed to persuade the cows to pass the body and as soon as they were safely in the milking parlour at the farm, Fred went to his boss, Mr Whitehouse, to tell him of his gruesome find. Whitehouse immediately sent his son, Thomas, to ride to Chester Road police station to summon the police to the scene.

The police acted quickly and, within the hour, they had closed all the roads leading out of the town, placing officers at key points to talk to any people trying to leave the area.

The body was that of an elderly woman, who, it seemed, had been the victim of an unimaginably savage attack. The woman was almost naked and had been beaten, stabbed, slashed and gouged from her head down to her knees. There were more than twenty stab wounds on her face and neck alone and she had a broken nose and two black eyes. Her face was ridged with scratches and deep puncture wounds, some of which appeared to have been done with a fork. The woman's throat was slashed, severing her jugular vein, and there were chunks of flesh carved from her chest. A gaping 7in-long wound crossed her abdomen and her left leg had been all but severed. The tops of her thighs were blackened with bruises, as was her face and also the backs of her hands, as if she had desperately fought her attacker.

A small, bloody knife lay on top of her body and, a few feet away, was a bent fork. Although neither was large enough to have made all of the dead woman's wounds, it appeared that both had been used against her.

The body lay in a pool of blood and a hollow in the grass nearby was also filled with blood and had been covered by a black shawl in order to hide it. The verges showed signs of a frantic struggle, extending 50 yards or so down the lane, where the tattered remnants of a black bonnet were found. Marks in the soft earth indicated that the woman had been dragged a considerable distance from the first point of attack to her final resting place.

The woman's possessions were widely scattered around her body. They included a Roman Catholic Bible, a clay pipe and some coloured matches. Two cards were also found close by, which turned out to be identity cards, from which it was established that the dead woman had recently worked as a hop picker at two local farms. The cards also gave her name – Mary Swinbourne.

As soon as news of the murder spread around the area, people flocked in droves to view the site. Mary's body was removed to a stable at Aggborough Farm and Mr Whitehouse blocked the entrance to the lane where she had been discovered with gates. He and his son-in-law manned the gates for several days, charging people 1d admittance to view the scene, the proceeds being donated to the local hospital.

Mary's remains were examined and it was found that, in the few areas where her body was still covered by clothes, her flesh was still warm. Thus it was determined that she had most probably met her death at around midnight on 3/4 October.

Hop pickers in Worcestershire, 1905. (Auhor's collection)

Her underclothes bore the stamp of the workhouse at Walsall and, when police visited there, they found that she had been an inmate, although she occasionally lived with her son in Walsall. Mary had given birth to thirteen children, nine of whom survived her. Her husband had deserted her, leaving Mary to do whatever she could to feed and clothe her brood. When things got too much for her, she turned to alcohol for solace and, in recent years, had become an alcoholic. Sixty-four-year-old Mary had been an inmate of the workhouse until 15 August, when she had discharged herself in order to go hop picking. She had last worked for a Mr Depper at Clifton-on-Teme on 2 October, earning 2s.

However, the hop-picking season was then all but over and Mary had written to her family saying that she didn't know what she was going to do next. When the police visited Mr Depper, they found that he had taken a party of his workers to the Rising Sun public house at Stourport. There he bought Mary a pint of beer and, when she told him that she was planning to go on to Kidderminster, had given her 3d for her fare. Mary had told him that she could go in a workman's car for half that price but he had insisted she take all the money. She was also given a knife and fork by a fellow hop picker who had originally intended to throw them away, since the fork was bent.

From the Rising Sun, Mary had gone to the Station Hotel and it was thought that she then walked the 3 miles or so to the Wren's Nest Inn. According to the landlord there, a woman had called at about seven o'clock in the evening of 3 October, saying that she was thirsty and asking for a glass of beer. She was given a drink of water and sat outside on a bench drinking it and smoking her pipe.

Kidderminster Town Hall, 1930. (Author's collection)

The woman had also begged a few matches from a young boy who lived nearby and been given some coloured matches of the kind that were later found near Mary's body.

The police issued her description, appealing for sightings of her, and were inundated with replies. Several people believed they had seen her leaving Stourport and that two men were then following her. A woman thought that she had spoken to someone resembling Mary at the end of Aggborough Lane, when she had been alone and walking towards Kidderminster. Added to alleged sightings of Mary were a number of reports of strange men in the area, including a foreign-looking man outside the Wren's Nest who had tried to pick up a married woman and a man with bloodstained clothes, who had been seen on a tram at Kinver. Another witness came forward to say that a man had asked him for directions to a police station, as he had found a dead body and wished to report it.

The police then received a number of reports and sightings of Mary, which, although each initially seemed promising, eventually led to a series of dead ends.

First, a farmer told them that a man and a woman had knocked on his door on the night of the murder, asking if they might sleep in one of his barns. He refused and the couple went on their way towards Stourbridge. The farmer believed that the woman bore a strong resemblance to Mary Swinbourne and, when he was taken to view the body, he positively identified it as the woman who had been seeking shelter for the night. He was able to give a good description of her male companion. Then, a young man, Percy Mallard, came forward to say that he and his girlfriend had been walking near the same farm at eight o'clock that evening when they had heard a woman's voice shouting, 'Oh, don't Bill.'

Mallard's girlfriend had been terrified. The young man had looked down the lane towards where the voice seemed to be coming from but, at that very moment, the moon had gone behind the clouds and he was unable to see anything at all in the darkness. Minutes later, a man on a bicycle had cycled past the young couple, wearing a light-coloured cycling suit with knickerbocker trousers, although he had not come from the direction of the scream.

A train driver, Charles Sparry, had been travelling on the line between Kidderminster and Stourport on 3 October and reported seeing a man and woman walking towards the farm. The woman had been drunk, said the engine driver, and the man had his arm around her waist and appeared to be supporting her.

With various sightings of Mary close to the same farm, at least one of which had been confirmed by the farmer who had viewed the body, coupled with an ear witness to a woman screaming in the area at the relevant time, the police thought that they had made a breakthrough in the case. However, it was not to be, as, a couple of days later, the farmer contacted them again to tell them that the man and woman had returned to the farmhouse. He had been mistaken and the body was not Mary.

Some bloodstained clothes were found about 3 miles out of Kidderminster, while a pair of trousers was found in the town itself. However, in both cases the police were able to trace the owners of the discarded clothing and eliminate them from their enquiries.

Another drunken woman had been seen in the company of a man, this time near Aggborough Farm, close to where Mary's body had been found. Once again, the informant, William Shingler, asked to look at the body and he too positively identified it as Mary. He was able to describe her gentleman friend as being fifty to sixty years old and small, although of average build, weighing between ten and eleven stones. Shingler put the man's height at around 5ft 5in and said that he had been wearing dark-coloured clothes, with a hat pulled down low over his forehead. Most distinctively, the man sported an almost white moustache. As the couple passed him, Shingler had heard the man say, 'Oh, my darling,' but he had not heard whether the woman had replied.

Three days after the murder, the police made an arrest, but the man they arrested was later released without charge. Another arrest was made at Malvern on the following day. The man apprehended bore a strong resemblance to Shingler's description of Mary's companion and also had some recent scratches on his face. He too was released without charge, having been able to prove that he was at work at the crucial time of Mary's murder. Next, a beggar, who was behaving aggressively, was arrested in Kinver, but he too was subsequently sent on his way. The Kinver police also traced the bloodstained man seen on the tram, who was eliminated after proving that the blood on his clothes resulted from a fight in Worcester.

With no viable suspects the case went cold, until the following January, when the police had what seemed like an amazing stroke of luck. On 2 January, a vagrant,

The Old Prison, Kinver, 1905. (Author's collection)

George Fisher, was arrested in Market Rasen, Lincolnshire and sentenced to ten days' imprisonment for begging. On his arrest, he was stripped for a bath, his clothes were searched and a notebook was found in his pocket. The prison warder gave the book a cursory glance but was then called away and, as soon as he had left the room, Fisher ripped a page out of the notebook and stuffed it into his mouth. Obviously finding the paper somewhat indigestible, Fisher soon took the page out of his mouth and concealed it under the bath. However, a prisoner on cleaning duties in the bathroom reported what he had seen to the warder on his return. The page was retrieved and on it was written: 'I murdered Mary Swinford [*sic*] on Saturday evening first in October at Kidderminster, Worcestershire. God help me. Murder will out some day.'

The victim's name was slightly different and, although the murder had been committed on a Saturday, the date had been on the 3 or 4, rather than 1 October. Even so, what was written in the notebook was close enough to the facts for the police to arrest Fisher and charge him with the wilful murder of Mary Swinbourne. 'There's some truth in that. I didn't intend you to have it,' Fisher said when confronted with the page, admitting that it had been torn from his notebook and was written in his handwriting. He then refused to say any more, telling the police, 'I have said too much already. You must prove it.'

A few days later, Fisher suddenly burst into tears and, when a warder asked him why he was crying, Fisher answered, 'A woman has been murdered in Aggborough Lane near Kidderminster. Her name was Mary Swinford [*sic*] and she used to be called Walsall Mary.'

Released from his prison sentence, Fisher was immediately re-arrested and transported to Worcester Gaol. Now, rather than being tearful, he seemed to be treating the investigations as a joke.

At Worcester, Charles Sparry and William Shingler both positively identified Fisher as the man they had seen with Mary Swinbourne. Another man told the police that Fisher had asked him for some hot water on the day after the murder. Fisher admitted that the knife found on Mary's body belonged to him, but said that he had lost it in Ledbury some days before the murder. He told the police that he wouldn't have admitted this fact had he known where the knife was ultimately found.

Standing trial for the murder, Fisher insisted that he didn't remember writing the confession in his notebook and, at the time of the murder, he had been in South Molton, Devon, working for a man named Thomas Vicary. Brought into court to identify his former employee, Vicary first said that he didn't recognise Fisher, but the judge suggested that Fisher should speak to Vicary. As soon as Fisher spoke, Vicary recognised his voice and immediately confirmed that the defendant had worked for him constantly between 18 September and 17 October. Another of Vicary's employees testified that, on the night of the murder in Kidderminster, Fisher was with him, unloading trucks at the railway station in South Molton.

Lydia Taylor told the court that, while in South Molton, Fisher had lodged at her father's home and, on 5 October, had been asked to look after the house while her father was away.

The counsel for the defence then queried the identification of George Fisher as the man who was with Mary on the night that she died. Not only was it dark, he said, but also, at the time of the murder, George Fisher's appearance was quite different to now. A barber from South Molton was called to tell the court that, at the beginning of October 1903, Fisher's hair and moustache had been neatly trimmed.

In his summary of the case for the jury, the presiding judge expressed grave doubts, saying that he would need much stronger evidence to find the case proven. He therefore suggested to the jury that they should acquit George Fisher, which they promptly did. On his release, Thomas Vicary took George Fisher back to South Molton, promising to find him a job.

With their most promising suspect now tried and pronounced 'Not Guilty', the police had no further leads to follow and the case went cold again. Then, in 1914, yet another vagrant confessed to the murder of Mary Swinbourne. This time he was Alfred Kimberley, a former resident of Kidderminster, who had moved to Canada since the murder and was now in prison there, having been arrested for begging.

Quite by chance, two other former Kidderminster men were in Canada at the time of Kimberley's confession, both of whom remembered him. Charles Robinson and Noel Moriarty visited Kimberley in the Canadian prison and told the police that, at the time of the murder, he had been apprenticed to a plumber. He had been a 'good, steady lad' but had turned to drink immediately after the murder, eventually leaving England for America.

Kimberley's confession was widely viewed as an attempt to obtain a free passage back to England and, as he had only been nineteen or twenty years old at the time of the murder and didn't match the descriptions of the elderly man seen with Mary, he was left to his fate in Canada.

Thus, although the police received two confessions, the murder of Mary Swinbourne remains unsolved to this day.

18

'HE WENT AT ME WITH GREAT REVENGE'

Worcester, 1905

On 4 October 1905, Mrs Sarah Ann Staite was standing outside her house in the Moors, Worcester, casually chatting to her neighbour, forty-two-year-old Annie Yarnold, when a man suddenly walked through Mrs Yarnold's front gate. Looking up from her task of brushing her windowsills with a hand brush, Mrs Yarnold greeted the man with the words ,'What brings you here? How white you are.'

Mrs Staite heard no reply but saw the man sneer at her neighbour. Then Mrs Yarnold, who was widely known as 'Tippy-toe Nance' due to having a slight limp, walked towards her front door and reached around the edge of it, as if groping for the key. As she did so, the man silently stepped up behind her and struck a single blow on her back.

He immediately ran away and Mrs Staite rushed forward to help her neighbour, catching her as she collapsed and lowering her gently to the ground. Only then did she notice the handle of a knife protruding from Annie Yarnold.

Mrs Staite screamed for assistance and one of the first people to respond was Mr Frank Thomas, the licensee of the nearby York House Inn. Thomas grabbed the protruding knife with both hands and tried to extricate it from Annie Yarnold but such was the force of the blow that the knife had penetrated her body to a depth of 4in and its removal proved difficult. Thomas braced his knee against Mrs Yarnold in an attempt to get more purchase and finally succeeded in removing the knife, at which Annie began to bleed very heavily. Thomas then rushed back to his pub for brandy, which he poured down Annie's throat as she lay face up on her front yard.

The police were called and quickly arrived in a cab, having briefly stopped at the hospital on the way to collect a doctor. Dr Harris and Inspector Peacock loaded

Mrs Yarnold into the cab, still bleeding heavily, and took her to Worcester Royal Infirmary, where she underwent an immediate operation to try to halt her blood loss. However, the knife had penetrated her spinal column, causing partial paralysis and, after the surgery, Annie Yarnold had great difficulty in breathing.

Back at her house, the chief constable of Worcester was busy organising a search party consisting of half the city police force. Annie's attacker had quickly been identified as her estranged husband, William Yarnold, and it was initially feared that he might have committed suicide, as he was nowhere to be found. However, at eight o'clock that evening, Constable Evans came across him wandering on Droitwich Road in a dazed condition. Yarnold put up no resistance when Evans confronted him and made an arrest. Charged with the attempted murder of his wife, Yarnold asked Constable Evans, 'Is it me or the man she is living with?'

Annie was still clinging to life at the hospital, but such was the gravity of her condition that it was decided that she should give a deposition, which she did on 5 October, with William Yarnold in attendance. Having first stated that she understood that she was dangerously ill and unlikely to recover, Annie Yarnold stated that she had been stabbed between five and six o'clock on the previous afternoon. She identified her attacker as her estranged husband, saying, 'He went at me with great revenge,' and telling the magistrate taking her deposition that the stabbing had been '… savage, as if to kill me.' She then went on to describe the hitherto turbulent relationship between herself and the man she had been married to for fifteen or sixteen years.

Forty-eight-year-old William Yarnold had been a soldier and had served both in India and at the Boer War in South Africa. While he was away from home, his wife had found another man, George Miles, and had moved in with him. On Yarnold's return to England, his wife had briefly gone back to live with him, but their reunion had lasted less than a week before Annie left him again for Miles. According to Annie, her marriage to William had been an unhappy one – he had often beaten her and refused to work, forcing her into prostitution to support him.

Although it had been more than two years since Annie and William had parted, it seemed that William was not able to forget. The couple had bumped into each other several times in the recent past, either in the street or in a public house and, according to Annie, William had always tried to initiate a conversation on these occasions and had occasionally threatened her.

They had last met on 4 October, the day of the attack, at the Hope and Anchor public house in Worcester, where Annie was enjoying a peppermint cordial. On this occasion, no conversation had passed between them, although Annie stated that William 'looked very queer'. When William visited the toilet at the pub, Annie had left and had not seen her husband again until he unexpectedly arrived on her doorstep later that day and stabbed her.

Questioned by William at the end of her deposition, Annie admitted that George Miles had often come to her house while she was still living with her husband and, on occasions, William had hidden in the closet while Miles was at his house.

Annie died a few days later. The knife injury to her spinal cord, which was three quarters severed, had left her completely paralysed on her right-hand side and partially paralysed on her left. Thus, she had largely lost the use of the muscles that controlled her breathing and, as a result, her lungs had become congested, a development that ultimately proved fatal. On her death, William Yarnold was immediately charged with her wilful murder, this time making no reply to the charge against him.

Having been committed by magistrates to stand trial at the next Worcestershire Assizes, William Yarnold appeared before Mr Justice Kennedy on 18 November 1905. Described in the contemporary newspaper accounts of the trial as a man of 'quite soldierly aspect', Yarnold stood almost rigidly to attention as he pleaded 'Not Guilty' to the charge of wilful murder in a firm voice.

The prosecution team of Mr Farrant and the Hon. R. Coventry opened the proceedings by calling on Mrs Sarah Staite to relate what she had seen. She was followed into the witness box by a passer-by who had also seen the stabbing, although not quite as closely as Mrs Staite. Mrs Edith Stone had seen a man wearing a cap and a red muffler approach Mrs Yarnold, stab her and then run away. Although she had not seen the man's face, she clearly remembered the red muffler he had been wearing at the time. Yarnold had been wearing a red muffler on his arrest and had continued to wear it at his appearances at the magistrate's court, although he did not wear it at his trial.

Pub landlord Frank Thomas told the court of his attempts to administer first aid to Mrs Yarnold and of his struggle to pull the knife from her back. 'I had to push her away in an almost brutal manner and then pull with all my might to get it out,' he stated.

Worcester in the 1950s. (Author's collection)

Thomas had also seen Mrs Yarnold's attacker fleeing the scene and he too commented on the bright red muffler that the man had been wearing.

The next witness was John Payne, a farmer's son from Bosbury. Although William Yarnold was described in court as a rag-and-bone man, he had spent several weeks prior to the murder hop picking at the farm owned by Payne's father. Now Payne identified the murder weapon as the knife he had seen the defendant using in the course of his work, describing it as a five-inch butcher's knife with a string-bound handle.

Inspector Peacock was then called to the witness box and Mr Hardy, the counsel for the defence, questioned him at great length about Annie Yarnold's dying deposition. An intense legal argument followed about the admissibility of the declaration and, at one point, Yarnold appeared so bored by the discussion that, without consulting anybody, he abruptly turned on his heel and left the dock, descending to the cells below. Since the proceedings couldn't continue in his absence, he was quickly brought back and, after much debate between the counsels on original and duplicate copies, prosecuting counsel Mr Coventry stated that he had served adequate notice on Yarnold that the deposition was to be taken and the judge finally ruled that it could be read in court.

Mr Hardy immediately objected to the inclusion of that part of the deposition in which Mrs Yarnold spoke of events that had occurred two years prior to the murder. However, Mr Justice Kennedy overruled his objection, saying that while he could not exclude part of the deposition, he was sure that the jury would appreciate that any threats allegedly made so long ago would have lost all their effect after such a long period of time.

The court then heard from Mr V.G. Heseltine, the house surgeon at the infirmary, who had operated on Annie Yarnold and later performed the post-mortem examination on her body, finding her death to be due to congestion of the lungs, resulting from the paralysis caused by the knife wound. Mr Hardy then cross-questioned the surgeon on the operation, asking him if it was considered a risky procedure. When Mr Heseltine admitted that it was, Hardy asked if it were possible that the operation itself might have accelerated Annie Yarnold's death. Heseltine told the court that, while the operation had not actually prolonged Mrs Yarnold's life, it had not accelerated her death, but had made her more comfortable. Prior to the operation, she had been complaining of severe pain in her leg but her complaints ceased after she had been operated on.

It was then left to the opposing counsels to summarise the case. Mr Farrant, for the prosecution, took only three minutes to tell the jury that they could have no doubt that the accused had inflicted the wound that had caused Mrs Yarnold's death and that this was not something that had been done on the spur of the moment, in the heat of passion. On the contrary, Yarnold had deliberately gone to the house with the specific intention of killing his estranged wife, leaving no doubt in anyone's mind that the correct charge against him was one of wilful murder rather than manslaughter.

Mr Hardy began his summary for the defence by asking the jury to put aside anything that they might have read about the case and focus solely on the evidence they had heard today in court. He argued that this was a classic case of manslaughter. Yarnold was described by all who knew him as a quiet man with an unblemished military record. While he was away, his wife had lived with George Miles, all the while continuing to benefit from receiving Yarnold's pay, part of which would undoubtedly have been spent on Miles.

On Yarnold's return home from South Africa, Annie had gone back to him, staying only until his pay arrears had been spent, before going back to George Miles.

Although William Yarnold frequently visited public houses, he was not known to be a big drinker and nobody had ever heard him make any threats towards Annie, even though she had stated in her deposition that he had threatened her in the past. Mr Hardy maintained that, on the day of the murder, Yarnold had simply wanted to talk to his wife and that she had jumped to the conclusion that he was trying to get into her house and had grabbed for the door key to prevent him from doing so. Hardy reminded the jury that, in her deposition, Annie Yarnold herself had said that she had not felt herself to be in danger otherwise she would have got away. It had been Annie who had become 'agitated' and, determined to prevent him from entering the house, she who had rushed at her husband with the intention of striking him. Hardy dismissed Mrs Staite's eyewitness account, saying that perhaps she had only heard half the conversation between the Yarnolds and had not seen Annie rush at William.

Hardy then asked the jury to consider whether or not the operation had accelerated Annie Yarnold's death, telling them that if they had the slightest concerns on that question, they should return the minor verdict of manslaughter. Curiously, Mr Hardy made no reference to the removal of the knife from Annie Yarnold's back by Frank Thomas. Although he undoubtedly believed that he was helping the injured woman, Thomas's efforts to help could easily have contributed to the severity of her injuries, especially as she had only begun bleeding profusely once the knife was removed.

In his final summary of the case, Mr Justice Kennedy stated that, having reviewed the evidence in great detail, he had failed to find anything that could be called provocation in the eyes of the law. He explained provocation to the jury as 'the heating of the human blood to a point that a person was deprived of self control', stressing that although Annie Yarnold had both deceived and wronged her husband, that in itself was no justification for taking her life, particularly since a deadly weapon had been used to do so.

Addressing the question of murder and manslaughter, he told the jury that the defence had suggested that Annie's death was more down to the operation she had undergone than to the stabbing. If it had been proved that the operation was unnecessary or that it had been ineptly performed, then the responsibility of the prisoner in the death of his wife would be reduced. However, the evidence of the doctor in this case suggested that he had done everything in his power for Mrs Yarnold.

The jury deliberated for just ten minutes before returning a verdict of 'Guilty of Murder' against William Yarnold, although they tempered the verdict with a recommendation of mercy on the grounds of Annie Yarnold's co-habitation with George Miles. The clerk of the court then asked William Yarnold if he had anything to say before he was sentenced, but Yarnold did not reply. He showed less emotion than the judge, who appeared very much affected as he passed the death sentence.

As he awaited his fate in Worcester Prison, William Yarnold was unaware of the strenuous efforts to save his life, which led to a petition bearing almost 6,000 signatures being presented to the Home Secretary. Only when the Home Secretary declined to intervene with the due course of the law was Yarnold told about the petition. He broke down briefly and thanked everyone who had laboured on his behalf, saying that he was disappointed but fully prepared for his death and that he hoped that he would meet his wife and his friends again in Heaven. He was putting all his trust in Christ, who had paid the price for his sins.

Shortly before his death, Yarnold thanked the prison staff for their kindness towards him, in particular the prison chaplain, Revd R.R. Needham. Expressing regret for making 'a shipwreck' of his life, Yarnold asked that a message be sent to his 'pals' on Newport Street, telling them to 'put themselves right with God.'

Wearing a blue suit, although without his customary red muffler, William Yarnold approached the gallows almost willingly, walking briskly and holding himself erect, not requiring the assistance of the two prison warders who flanked him. The highly efficient Henry Pierrepoint carried out the execution, assisted by John Ellis and the chimes of eight o'clock had barely ceased when the prison bell rang out, signifying Yarnold's death. His was the first execution to be carried out at Worcester Prison for one hundred years.

Before his death, William Yarnold made out a formal will, in which he bequeathed the proceeds of an insurance policy to the infirmary. Although the sum was relatively small, amounting to only a few pounds, Yarnold reasoned that, having done so much harm in the world, he was glad to be able to do just a little good before he died.

19

'I CONSIDER HE IS A PERFECTLY SANE MAN'

Worcester, 1925

At seven o'clock on the morning of Friday 27 November 1925, charwoman Florence Hardwick arrived at her job at the Garibaldi Inn in Wyld's Lane, Worcester to find the pub in disarray and seemingly deserted. Although she could see no smoke, an unmistakeable smell of burning permeated the building. Mrs Hardwick called out several times but nobody answered. Concerned, she ran to neighbours for assistance and was accompanied back to the pub by Daniel Oram.

Together with Mrs Hardwick, Oram began to search for her employers, eventually going down into the pub's cellar, where the source of the foul, smoky smell immediately became apparent. On the cellar floor lay the bodies of the landlord, thirty-one-year-old Ernest George Elton Laight, and his wife Doris 'Dolly' Sabrina Laight, aged thirty. Both bodies were superficially charred, having been covered in paper, which had then been set alight, presumably to try and destroy the bodies and, with them, any evidence of the killer's identity.

Knowing that the Laights had two young children, Oram and Mrs Hardwick rushed upstairs to the bedrooms. There they found six-year-old Joan, still fast asleep in bed and mercifully completely unharmed. Her two-year-old brother, Robert, lay face down in his cot, sadly dead.

Joan was carried out of the house and was later placed in the care of relatives. The police were called, along with Dr Edward Walpole Simmons, who spent much of the morning examining the bodies. When he left the pub, the doctor was asked his opinion on the causes of death. 'I cannot say. It is a complete mystery,' he replied, sparking off a host of conflicting theories in the neighbourhood. The local newspaper, *Berrow's Worcester Journal*, gave voice to some of the rumours in their evening edition, stating that it was believed that the deaths were due to poisoning.

According to the newspaper, there were no marks of violence on any of the bodies, although some local people insisted that the head of at least one had been 'battered in' and speculated that robbery had been the motive for the killings. 'There is no ground for these stories,' stated the newspaper.

The Laights were an extremely popular family with no known enemies. Ernest had taken over the Garibaldi Inn in April 1925, prior to which he had run a busy baker's shop in New Street. A talented amateur footballer, he was known as a friendly, good-humoured man. He had been married to Dolly for about eight years and the marriage seemed a happy one. Drinkers in the pub on the night before the murders told the police that both of the Laights had been behaving normally and there was no hint of any quarrel between them. None of the neighbours had seen or heard anything unusual during the night.

Post-mortem examinations were carried out on the three bodies, resolving the mystery of how they met their deaths. Mr and Mrs Laight had both been shot in the chest; the gunshot wounds had initially been disguised by the charring on their bodies. In both cases, a single bullet had penetrated the heart and lung and Mr Laight had an additional gunshot wound to his left eye. Young Bobby Laight was found to have a fractured skull. Meanwhile, a search of the pub revealed a pair of rubber gloves lying at the top of the cellar steps. The drawer had been removed from the till and lay empty on the floor, along with a scattering of copper coins and slot machine tokens.

Even as the police began their investigations into the mysterious deaths of the Laight family, a chance remark appeared to have solved the case for them. Between half-past seven and eight o'clock on the morning after the murders, a probationary police constable, Herbert Burrows, approached a colleague, Constable William Devy, complaining of feeling ill with pains around his heart and asking where he might get some brandy. Burrows then asked Devy if he had heard about the 'affair' at the Garibaldi in Wyld's Lane.

When Constable Devy said that he had heard nothing, Burrows went on to tell him that Mr Laight and his wife had been found shot in the cellar, with one of the 'kiddies' dead in his bed. Devy asked Burrows how he knew and Burrows replied, 'A man told me.' Ten minutes later, Burrows raised the subject again, telling Devy that he had been drinking with Mr Laight at midnight and had probably been the last person to see him before he was killed.

The two policemen ate breakfast together and once again Burrows began talking about the case, asking his colleague if he thought it would prevent him from going on his planned leave to London. 'Don't be silly,' replied Devy. 'Do you think the police force can't do without you?' At that, the subject was dropped and Devy thought no more about it until more details of the case gradually filtered into the police station. Only then did Devy realise that Burrows had actually been talking about the murders in some detail before the police had officially known about them. They had first been informed at the police station at 9 a.m. that Mr and Mrs Laight had been shot, yet Burrows seemed to have known their fate at least an hour before. As a result, Devy went straight to Detective Sergeant Fisher to report his strange conversations with Burrows.

Burrows should have gone off duty at two o'clock on the afternoon of 27 November, when he was planning to catch a train to London to see his parents and to finalise arrangements for his forthcoming marriage to a girl who worked for a London drapery company. Instead he found himself being interviewed by Detective Sergeant Fisher about his detailed knowledge of the Garibaldi Inn murders. Following the interview, Burrows' lodgings were searched.

He rented rooms in Wyld's Lane, almost opposite the Garibaldi Inn, where he was known to be a regular drinker. When Fisher searched his bedroom, he found an unlicensed, fully loaded American revolver in a locked drawer, along with a box of cartridges and three empty cartridge cases. In a suitcase under the bed, Fisher found thirty-four £1 notes, twenty-six 10s notes and more than £22 in silver coins, along with some slot machine tokens. Finally, the detective found receipts and paperwork apparently indicating that Burrows was in considerable debt to a moneylender.

Herbert Burrows was arrested and, at 4 p.m. on 27 November, was formally charged with the murders of the Laight family. He immediately confessed, saying, 'I voluntarily and fully admit that I killed at 12.50 a.m. on the 27th Mr and Mrs Laight and Robert Laight. The cause will remain unknown. I apologize to the officers and men of the Worcester City Police for the disgrace thus incurred.' When Burrows was searched on his arrest, a further £17 10s in notes was found on his person, along with more silver coins.

Wyld's Lane, Worcester. (© N. Sly, 2008)

Burrows appeared before magistrates at the Guildhall, Worcester on 4 December 1925. Undefended, he was committed for trial at the next Assizes. When asked if he had anything to say in reply to the charges against him, Burrows said that he wished only to clear up one point; the money found on him when he was searched after his arrest was his own money, which he had saved from his wages for his leave. The money in the suitcase in his bedroom had been stolen from two cash boxes in the upstairs room of the pub.

The trial opened on 27 January 1926 before Mr Justice Sankey, with Mr Geoffrey Lawrence and Mr Guy Lailey prosecuting and Mr A.F. Clements defending. Twenty-three-year-old Herbert Burrows pleaded not guilty.

In view of his confession to the murders, there was little doubt in anyone's mind that Burrows had killed all three members of the Laight family. Finding himself short of money and in debt, he had stayed after hours at the pub on the night of Friday 27 November, enjoying a glass of whisky. He had shot Ernest Laight in the pub cellar and, when Dolly had come to investigate the noise, he had shot her too, dragging her body next to her husband's. Young Robert was killed in case his crying alerted people to a problem at the pub. The prosecution theorised that Burrows had woken the boy as he passed through his bedroom in search of the pub's cashboxes, which were kept in a back bedroom. When the boy cried at being disturbed, Burrows had hit him on the head, fracturing his skull.

With so strong a case against the accused, his only hope was a defence of insanity, and it was this angle that his counsel pursued in court. Burrows had joined the Worcester City Police after a spell in the Navy and was six months into his twelve-month probationary period at the time of the murders. The defence produced evidence that Burrows was suffering from syphilis and was displaying some of the symptoms of nervous degeneracy associated with the disease.

However, the prosecution refuted any suggestions of insanity, maintaining that the murder of the Laight family was cold-blooded and premeditated, with robbery as its motive. It had taken place at the end of a month, a time when Mr Laight would have been expected to have a large amount of cash on the premises. Indeed, the brewery had estimated that there would have been around £80 of takings at the pub awaiting banking – an almost identical amount to that found in Burrows' possession after his arrest.

The end of the month of November had coincided with Burrows' planned leave and there was evidence that he was in debt. He had deliberately gone to the pub with a revolver and ammunition with the sole intention of robbery. Not only that, but he had had the presence of mind to take rubber gloves with him, knowing as a policeman that any fingerprints that he left at the scene could be traced back to him.

The prosecution and defence counsels then called a series of medical witnesses to give their opinions on the sanity or otherwise of the accused.

Burrows had been held in Gloucester Prison pending his trial since 29 November, during which time he had been under observation by Dr Bell, the medical officer.

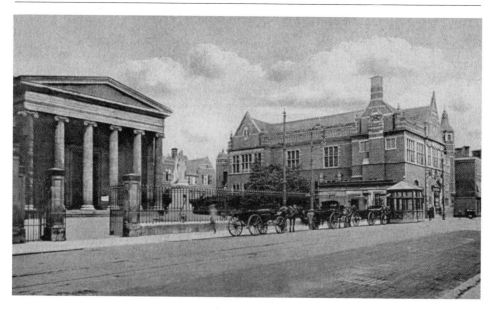

Shire Hall and Institute, Worcester, 1920s. (Author's collection)

'I consider he is a perfectly sane man,' stated Dr Bell, although he conceded that there were some apparent symptoms of nervous degeneracy associated with syphilis. Burrows had described the killings to Dr Bell in great detail and, at no time had he shown any remorse for his actions.

Dr Smith of Winson Green Prison in Birmingham disagreed. He had been asked to examine Burrows and had also been told about the killings by the accused. Smith felt that the defendant's demeanour while relating the details of the crime was indicative of mental abnormality and he believed that Burrows was in the early stages of general paralysis as a result of his syphilitic status. Dr Fenton, of Powick Mental Asylum, concurred with Smith's opinion.

It was left to Mr Justice Sankey to sum up the case for the jury, paying particular attention to the legalities of the insanity defence. He then adjourned the court for lunch, asking the jury to consider their verdict and, by the time the court reconvened thirty minutes later, the jury had decided that Herbert Burrows was guilty of all three charges of murder against him.

Burrows showed no emotion as Sankey sentenced him to death, standing rigidly to attention while the sentence was pronounced. He refused to allow his counsel to appeal his conviction and was executed at Gloucester Prison on 17 February 1926 by Thomas Pierrepoint, who was assisted by William Wills.

Before his death, he composed a letter to Doris Laight's mother, in which he stressed that the rumours of an affair between him and Dolly were completely untrue.

20

'LOOK HOW SHE HAS SERVED ME OUT'

At about half-past nine on the evening of Sunday 5 July 1925, Mrs Millie Pardoe was walking through Lye when she noticed a man behaving very strangely at the entrance to the brickyard of Messrs Hickman & Co. The man was in his shirtsleeves and the entire front of his body was saturated with blood, which dripped onto the ground from his arms and hands. As Mrs Pardoe approached him, he told her, 'There's a woman down there who has cut her throat.'

The man calmly led Mrs Pardoe through the brickyard, chatting to her as they walked as though they were out for a pleasant evening stroll. He told her that the woman was his stepsister, Alice, and that she was dead. 'She went to the drawer and took out a razor and ran outside,' said the man. 'I went after her and we struggled and I kicked the razor from her hand.' He then pointed down to his bloodstained clothes and body and said, 'Look how she has served me out,' as if it were somehow the woman's fault that he was now covered in her blood.

Before long, they came to the body of a young woman, stretched out on the yard in a large pool of blood, her throat slashed from ear to ear. Before Mrs Pardoe could react, an older woman suddenly ran screaming out of a house at the side of the brickyard. The hysterical woman exchanged a few words with the blood-soaked man, who afterwards ran out of the yard.

A doctor was called, even though it was blatantly obvious that the would-be suicide had succeeded in what she set out to do. However, when Dr H.C. Darby arrived and had had a chance to examine the dead woman, he immediately ruled out suicide as the cause of her death. The slash to her throat stretched from ear to ear and had penetrated almost to her backbone and the doctor was in no doubt whatsoever that somebody who was both strong and muscular had inflicted the terrible injury, while standing behind the woman. Furthermore, when the doctor was able to examine the young woman's body more closely, he found that she had been dreadfully mutilated, with at least thirty incised wounds on her neck, breasts, genitalia and thighs.

The hysterical older woman was the mother of the deceased girl. Now, almost insensible with grief, she was taken back to her cottage on the edge of the brickyard, where she was able to give the police some information about the dead girl and the young man who had fled the scene.

The distraught woman was Ellen Checketts and she shared the cottage with her husband, James, and her children. The deceased girl was Alice Mary Rowley, aged twenty-two, who was Ellen's daughter from a previous marriage. The young man was Alice's stepbrother, Bert, aged twenty-four, an unemployed labourer, who was James's son by a former marriage. Ellen told the police that she believed that Bert had been in love with Alice but that her daughter had ignored his attentions. On occasions, Bert had even followed Alice around like a lost puppy, but she was immune to his advances. Bert had desperately wanted Alice to love him and, when she didn't return his affection, he had exacted his revenge by destroying some of her clothes and burying four of her hats.

On the day before the murder, Bert and Alice had argued after Bert had asked Alice to lend him sixpence and Alice told him that she didn't have the money to lend him. The argument had reached such a pitch that Robert Collins, a passer-by, had felt bound to intervene to see Alice home safely. Bert had obviously born a grudge, since, on the day of the murder, he appeared to sulk all day and barely spoke to his stepsister until that evening, when he had apparently taken his razor to her throat.

Bert Checketts was quickly apprehended and taken into custody. He expressed surprise at being arrested, telling the police that he was innocent. 'She did it herself,' he insisted. 'I happened to look through the window and saw her using the razor. She cut herself in three or four places and I thought it was my duty to go out and stop her.'

Bert Checketts appeared before magistrates at Stourbridge Police Court on 17 July, charged with Alice's murder, and was committed for trial at the Autumn Assizes in Worcester. His trial opened on 23 October 1925 before Mr Justice Roche. The prosecution counsel was Mr G.K. Rose, while Dr Earengey defended Checketts, who pleaded 'Not Guilty' to the charge of murder against him.

It quickly became evident that the crux of the proceedings would be the question of whether or not Bert Checketts was insane at the time of the murder. After Mrs Pardoe testified about her involvement in the discovery of Alice Rowley's body, the next witness to take the stand was Ellen Checketts.

Ellen told the court that, on the night of the murder, she had seen her daughter lying in the yard and had heard somebody say, 'He's killed her.' She then remembered nothing at all until the following morning. Dr Earengey asked her if she had ever known her stepson to behave strangely in the past and she replied that Bert often came into the house laughing and would not stop. By now, the strain of giving her

Stourbridge Road, Lye. (© N. Sly, 2008)

evidence was obviously becoming unbearable for Ellen and the defence counsel took pity on her, suggesting that he could direct his questions to her husband at a later stage of the trial. The distressed mother was then led from the court in a state of near collapse, to be replaced in the witness box by Dr Darby.

Darby detailed the terrible injuries and mutilation that Alice had suffered and repeated his opinion that the fatal wound to her throat had been inflicted from behind and could therefore not have been made by her own hand. The doctor had made detailed drawings, cataloguing the girl's wounds, and these were passed to the jury for their inspection.

Under questioning from Dr Earengey, he admitted that the number and character of Alice's wounds suggested that they were the work of a person whose mind was abnormal. 'Probably done by a person in a state of frenzy?' asked the defence counsel, to which Darby replied that a person in a state of frenzy might develop temporary insanity.

Dr Earengey then went on to ask Dr Darby about a visit he had made to see Bert Checketts during the previous December. The defence counsel seemed very reticent to probe too far into the reasons for this visit and Dr Darby was just as unwilling to answer. Eventually, Mr Justice Roche intervened to say that, while he understood their discomfort, the information was essential in understanding the case.

Darby finally admitted that he had been called in by Bert Checketts' parents to see the defendant because of 'certain revolting practices' that Bert had been engaging in. Darby had admonished him and was later told by Mr and Mrs Checketts that their son seemed to have taken some notice of the admonishments and that, as a result, his behaviour had improved. Dr Earengey asked Darby if he had formed an opinion about the accused's mental state at this time and Darby replied that he believed that Bert was certainly feeble-minded, but that he did not regard him as a certifiable lunatic.

A gasp of astonishment echoed around the court as the next witness took the stand. Mr C.G. Duncan, the county analyst, had been sent Alice Rowley's organs for examination and stated that they had shown evidence of 'intimate association with a man.'

James Checketts was next to be called and stated that his son had always behaved very strangely towards Alice Rowley. Bert had wanted to make love to her, but Alice had always ignored his advances.

'Did he know the difference between right and wrong?' asked Mr Rose.

'Oh, yes,' James Checketts insisted.

The prosecution then called Robert Collins, who had gallantly assisted Alice Rowley during her argument with her stepbrother on the night before her death, after which Constable Nash and Constable Dadge told the court about Bert's arrest and subsequent detention. Mr Rose then said that he had concluded the case for the prosecution, unless the defence would like him to call the prison doctor, under whose charge Checketts had been since his arrest.

Dr Earengey stated that he intended to rely on a defence of insanity, at which the judge suggested that the prison doctor be called immediately.

Dr Hamblin Smith stated that he had observed Bert Checketts since July and had found him to be generally well behaved, although perhaps abnormally cheerful in the light of the gravity of his present situation. His conversation was quite childish and tended to include a great deal of unnecessary detail and he was at times very volatile. He had below average intelligence and had a very poor memory and it was quite possible that, if excited, he might lose control of himself.

Questioned by Mr Rose, the doctor described Checketts' condition as 'a malformation of the mind', with a diminished power of reasoning. Whereas he knew the difference between right and wrong, in killing his stepsister he would not fully appreciate the seriousness of his actions.

At this point, the judge interrupted to ask, 'Is it a fact that in some men there survives what might be called the animal instinct of attacking the female in sexual excitement?'

Dr Smith agreed that this was true.

'Is it a known form of mental state?' the judge persisted.

'Yes.'

'There are indications here of the probability of that motive or passion being in operation?'

'I should say yes,' agreed Smith.

'And assuming that this man did what was done, is that, in your opinion, possibly or probably the explanation of what happened?'

'Yes. I think it's certainly possible. I think it is probable,' replied the doctor.

Having satisfied himself that he fully understood the medical evidence, Mr Justice Roche then reminded the court that they were bound by the McNaghten Rules.

These had arisen in 1843 after a man named Daniel McNaghten had shot and killed the secretary to the then Prime Minister, under the mistaken impression that the secretary was actually the Prime Minister, Sir Robert Peel. McNaghten was, at the time, suffering from a mental illness and believed that Peel was part of a plot to persecute and destroy him. From this case arose the McNaghten Rules, which stated that 'in order to establish a defence of insanity, it must be proved that the accused was labouring under such a defect of reason from disease of the mind as not to know the nature and quality of the act he was doing or, if he did know it, that he did not know that what he was doing was wrong.'

The judge then asked Dr Smith if he was of the opinion that this case came within any of the McNaghten Rules.

'I would think it would hinge upon the precise meaning attached to the premise of knowing the quality and nature of the act,' replied Smith, adding that Bert Checketts would have certainly known that he was killing a woman.

'If that is the explanation, then this case certainly does not fall within the rules,' stated the judge, effectively negating Dr Earengey's insanity defence with that one sentence.

Nevertheless, when it was his turn to address the jury, Earengey insisted that his client was feeble-minded and had harboured a deep love for the victim, which had been unrequited. At the time of the murder, he had temporarily become a sexual maniac and did not know the nature of the act that he was committing in killing his stepsister. Citing the victim's 'ghastly mutilations' as evidence that no sane man could have committed the murder, Earengey asked the jury to return a verdict of 'Guilty but Insane'.

In his summary of the case, Mr Justice Roche stated that, in his judgement, according to the law of the land, there were insufficient grounds for such a verdict. The defendant obviously had low intelligence and diminished responsibility but the question of whether or not he was insane was debatable. Roche told the jury that if they returned a verdict of guilty, then there were people whose job it was to advise His Majesty the King whether sentence of death should be carried out and that he personally did not know what would be the outcome of a guilty verdict.

Given that Bert Checketts had been caught literally red-handed and that his razor had been found near his victim's body, the guilty verdict from the jury was a foregone conclusion. The judge then pronounced sentence of death on Bert Checketts, who seemed completely unmoved by his words.

In the event, those whose duty it was to advise the King obviously disagreed about the pertinence of the McNaghten rules to the case, as in November 1925 the sentence of death was commuted by the Home Secretary, who ordered that Bert Checketts be detained in a mental hospital pending His Majesty's pleasure.

Note: In some contemporary sources, Bert Checketts' first name is alternatively spelled Burt.

21

'COME ON, LET'S DIE TOGETHER'

Northfield, 1942

In July 1941, forty-year-old Harold Oswald Merry from Redditch began a new job at the Austin Motor Co. at Longbridge, doing vital war work as a sheet-metal inspector. Before too long, he found himself strongly attracted to Joyce Dixon, a shorthand typist at the factory.

The fact that Harold was a married man with five children, ranging in age from one to fourteen years old, didn't seem to matter to him as within weeks he was declaring himself in love with Joyce, who was thirteen years his junior. Harold's wife and family were so far from his mind that he had even neglected to tell Joyce of their existence, although in September 1941, Harold's foreman at work rectified this omission.

Joyce obviously accepted Harold's situation, probably seduced by promises that he would leave his wife, and she and Harold continued to see each other outside work. Harold even visited Joyce at the house in Northfield that she shared with her widowed mother, although Mrs Dixon was not told of Harold's marital status.

Towards the end of September, Harold's comfortable existence was suddenly thrown into turmoil when his wife intercepted a love letter that Joyce had written to him and sent to his house. A furious row ensued and Harold was thrown out of his marital home and forced to live with his sister, Lily Price, in Redditch. Even so, he continued to visit his wife and children on a weekly basis, usually taking the opportunity to have a bath and collect clean clothes for the following week. In spite of objections from his sister, Harold also continued to see Joyce.

In March 1942, Harold approached Joyce's mother, Kate Dixon, and asked for her permission to get engaged. 'We understand each other,' he explained and Kate told him that she had no objection to the arrangement if Harold and Joyce were happy.

Harold told her that he was shortly going to London on business and would be staying at the home of his niece's boyfriend's parents. He asked if he might take Joyce with him so that the couple could choose her engagement ring at one of the big London stores. Harold's wife was also told about the proposed business trip and, on the night before he left, Harold stayed with her at his old home.

The business trip and the accommodation were a complete fabrication and, once in London, Harold and Joyce booked into a hotel as 'Mr and Mrs Merry'. However, while they were enjoying their illicit relationship, Joyce's supervisor at work called on Kate Dixon and informed her that Harold was a married man. When the couple returned to Northfield, Joyce's mother confronted Harold, who immediately denied that he was married, telling Mrs Dixon that he had lied to his employers in order to get a job.

His explanation sounded so implausible to Mrs Dixon that she encouraged her daughter to work overtime at the factory so that she would have less time to spend with Harold. Meanwhile, Harold had fallen out with his sister, who had never approved of his extra-marital relationship with Joyce and, although she had taken him in when his wife threw him out, had issued several ultimatums to her brother to end his affair. Amazingly, when his sister asked him to leave her home, Harold then moved back in with his long-suffering wife.

On 29 March 1942, Joyce told her mother that she was meeting Harold as he owed her some money and she was hoping to get it back from him. The two met in Quinton Park in the late afternoon and what happened at that meeting can only be told from Harold's point of view, since Joyce failed to return from their final tryst.

According to Harold, Joyce was very upset and tearful about her mother's attitude to her since her return from London. Mrs Dixon kept asking questions about her daughter's relationship with Harold and Joyce was afraid that her mother didn't love her anymore. Harold told her that her mother would soon come round, but Joyce refused to be consoled. 'We cannot get married,' she allegedly told Harold, 'but we could die together.'

Harold tried to distract her with chocolate and oranges left over from their trip to London, both luxury items that had become very scarce during the war years. However Joyce persisted and eventually, at her insistence, Harold pulled a notebook from his pocket and penned a joint suicide note:

> Joyce and I have been living as man and wife at 36 Bloomsbury Street London, hoping that I should be able to get a divorce. We have been trying to keep it away from Joyce's mother, Mrs Dixon, but Joyce's foreman went and told Mrs Dixon I was married. So we find it impossible to carry on much longer. So we are going to die together because we are terribly in love with each other. We were going to London to live after the holidays, and find some more work, but since Joyce's foreman told Mrs Dixon it has upset our plans. Joyce herself knows I was married. I told her myself, also Mr Taylor, my foreman, told her last September and for God's sake forgive her. She is so happy now. She knows we are going to die together. So goodbye all. [*sic*]

Joyce read the note and signed it. 'I suppose when we get home we will have changed our minds,' Harold remarked.

'Yes, I suppose we will,' replied Joyce.

Harold walked Joyce back to her home and the couple kissed goodnight at the end of her road. Harold left Joyce there but, as soon as he started to walk away, she called him back, telling him that she could not go home. Harold offered to come with her and talk to her mother, but Joyce insisted that the couple followed their original plan and committed suicide. With no clear ideas about exactly how they were going to accomplish this, Harold and Joyce walked off again to the fields near her home.

Harold pleaded with Joyce to go home, but she was determined. 'Come on, let's die together,' she begged him and eventually Harold took the spare necktie that he habitually carried in his pocket and wrapped it around Joyce's neck.

He was later to insist that Joyce helped him to pull the tie tight around her throat but, in the event, the couple's plan was thwarted since the necktie broke as Harold pulled on it. Joyce slumped to the floor, still fully conscious. At that point the couple heard voices approaching.

Harold tried to pull Joyce to her feet, but she resisted. 'Let's go home to your mother,' Harold suggested, but Joyce refused. Eventually, Harold said that he climbed over a stile and walked into the next field, hoping that Joyce would follow him. She didn't and, after around ten minutes, he went back to look for her. There was no sign of her where he had left her, so he began to search for her. As he neared a pool at Turves Green Farm in Northfield, he saw something floating there and realised that it was Joyce.

Church Hill, Northfield. (Author's collection)

Harold immediately waded into the pool, but when he reached Joyce her found her dead. He removed the tie that he was wearing, put it round his own neck and pulled the ends hard, but once again the tie broke, leaving him feeling dazed and dizzy. He was still standing in the pool and eventually fainted, however the shock of the cold water quickly brought him round.

He went back to the bank and smoked a cigarette before wading back into the water, determined to kill himself. However, as he lay face down in the water, he thought of his children and heard a voice in his head saying, 'Don't do it.' He then tried to drag Joyce out of the pool, but found it impossible. He eventually left her lying in the water and went to his wife's house. What she said when he arrived on her doorstep dripping wet in the early morning of 30 March is not recorded.

Meanwhile Joyce Dixon's mother was frantic with worry. She telephoned Joyce's brother, Victor, at half-past seven in the morning to tell him that his sister had gone for a walk the previous afternoon and had not returned. Victor Dixon telephoned the Longbridge works and, when he found out that neither his sister nor Harold Merry had reported for work that morning, he got straight in his car and drove to Merry's house.

Mrs Merry answered his knock on the door and shouted upstairs to tell her husband that he was wanted. As Dixon waited for him to come down, he heard a bumping noise coming from a bedroom. He raced upstairs and found Harold Merry standing with a length of electrical cord wrapped around his neck. Victor removed the cord and asked Harold where his sister was.

'I will take you to her,' replied Harold.

'You have murdered her,' said Victor.

'That's right. She's in the brook in the field at the back of the house.'

Dixon immediately bundled Harold Merry into his car and drove him to Redditch police station, where he told officers that Harold had murdered his sister. Constable Albert Morris was on duty at the time. He had known Harold Merry for twenty years and had always believed him to be a respectable man – the Harold Merry who stood before him now, damp and white faced, his teeth chattering from the cold, bore little resemblance to the man Morris had always known and he wondered if Merry might have had some sort of nervous breakdown. However, Merry seemed perfectly composed and rational. He was searched and the police found the damp notebook in his pocket containing the suicide letter signed by Joyce. They also found three love letters that she had written to him, which were filled with sentimental statements like 'I love you so terribly' and 'I love you with all my heart'.

Harold led the police to where Joyce's body still floated face downwards in the pool, fully clothed except for her shoes and hat. On his arrest, Harold seemed perfectly happy to admit his part in her death, telling the police, 'All I can say is that I am guilty.' However, three days later, he asked to make another statement, in which he told the police that he had thought things over and had now decided that he wasn't guilty.

The police called in Professor James Webster of the Forensic Laboratory at Birmingham, who performed a post-mortem examination on the body of Joyce Dixon. He first confirmed that Joyce hadn't been pregnant, before going on to pinpoint the cause of her death as asphyxia from drowning. Webster believed that Joyce had been strangled into unconsciousness and then deliberately placed in the water to drown.

Harold Merry was charged with her wilful murder and was tried at the Birmingham Assizes on 17 July 1942, before Mr Croom-Johnston. Paul F. Sandlands and Mr A.P. Marshall prosecuted the case, while John F. Bourke and Mr G.T. Meredith conducted Merry's defence.

The judge was known as a somewhat peppery man, who did not suffer fools gladly and, during the court proceedings, he made several remarks that, in hindsight, might be considered imprudent. When he caught the defendant smiling, he snapped at him, 'Don't smile about it, this is a serious matter,' and on another occasion he rounded on the counsel for the prosecution and asked, 'Haven't you asked enough questions?'

The court heard from the key witnesses in the case, including hotel manageress Doris Webster, who testified that 'Mr and Mrs Merry' had stayed at her premises in Bloomsbury Street between 21 and 27 March that year and that they had seemed very happy.

Professor Webster was also called to testify and in cross-examination by the counsel for the defence was questioned about his unshakeable assertion that Joyce Dixon had been unconscious when she entered the water. Webster conceded that it

Birmingham law courts, 1920s. (Author's collection)

was 'not beyond possibility' that Joyce was conscious when she was first immersed in water, but pointed out that it was not beyond theoretical possibility to fly to the moon, although he doubted its practicability.

It was known that Joyce Dixon had spent some time as a patient in a mental hospital in Rubery for what was described as 'a nervous breakdown', caused by overwork. She initially went into hospital in July 1931 and was discharged in February 1932. She was then readmitted in December 1935 and, this time, stayed until January 1937, when she was considered to be completely cured. The fact that the victim had a previous history of mental illness was given surprisingly scant attention in court, as was the 'suicide letter', which had definitely been signed by Miss Dixon. Instead, the defence counsel focused on trying to persuade the jury to return a verdict of attempted murder rather than one of wilful murder or manslaughter. Mr Bourke told the jury that Harold was 'a bad, immoral man' and, but for him, Joyce Dixon would almost certainly be alive. Hearing this, Merry began to weep quietly, showing the first signs of emotion that he had shown thus far in the proceedings.

He had recovered his composure in time to hear the jury return a verdict of 'Guilty of Wilful Murder' against him and, in the face of hysterical outbursts from the body of the court, stood calmly while the judge pronounced the sentence of death.

In the wake of his sentence, many people felt that he had been wrongly convicted, particularly as there was evidence of a suicide pact between the lovers, which indicated that Joyce Dixon had been both ready and willing to die.

As his defence counsel appealed his conviction on the grounds of what they believed to be a misdirection of the jury, the people of Redditch set about raising a petition for clemency, which eventually numbered 2,000 signatures.

However, the Court of Criminal Justice dismissed Merry's appeal on 26 August 1942 and the Home Secretary responded to the petition by declining to interfere in the course of justice. Thus, Harold Oswald Merry was hanged at Birmingham Prison on 10 September 1942 by Thomas Pierrepoint, who was assisted by Henry Critchell.

22

'WHO PUT BELLA IN THE WYCH ELM?'

Hagley Wood, 1943

A Sunday spent looking for bird's nests was a typical day's outing for teenagers Bob Farmer, Tom Willetts, Bob Hart and Fred Payne of Stourbridge, and, on 18 April 1943, the boys chose to spend the day exploring Hagley Wood, near the village of Hagley. They were coming to the end of their expedition when they decided to check just one more place before heading home – a large wych elm tree.

As the boys climbed the tree, Bob Farmer happened to look down into the trunk and saw what appeared to be a human skull looking up at him. Unsure about whether or not they should have been in the woods in the first place, the four boys decided to say nothing about their macabre find. However, Tommy Willetts, the youngest of the four, was unable to keep the secret and later told his father what he thought he had seen. Mr Willetts went straight to the police.

Sergeant Skerrett was sent to the scene and, having confirmed the boys' find, placed the tree under police guard until first light. The following morning, the skeletal remains of a woman were removed from the hollow tree and sent to pathologist Professor James M. Webster, of the Home Office Laboratory of Forensic Science at Birmingham, for investigation.

The woman had obviously been dead for some time and the skeleton removed from inside the tree was far from complete. However, a fingertip search of the surrounding undergrowth revealed still more body parts, including a severed hand, buried a few feet away from the tree.

Professor Webster set about reassembling the skeleton and was eventually able to give the police a remarkably detailed description of the mystery woman. According to Webster, she was approximately thirty-five years old and had probably borne at

NOTICEABLE IRREGULARITY FRONT TEETH, LOWER JAW

HEIGHT ABT. 5 FT.

BROWN HAIR

DARK BLUE STRIPED KNITTED WOOLLEN CARDIGAN

LIGHT BLUE BELT

AGE ABT. 35

MOCK WEDDING RING (VALUE 2/6

CLOTH SKIRT WITH ZIP

PEACH COLOURED TAFFETA UNDER SKIRT

BLUE, CREPE SOLED SHOES

An artist's impression of the victim. (Courtesy of the Express and Star, *Wolverhampton)*

least one child. About 5ft tall, she had mousy brown hair and distinct irregularities in the teeth of her lower jaw.

Remnants of the woman's clothes were found with her body and Professor Webster was able to describe her outfit to the police as a mustard coloured skirt with a side zip fastening, a woollen cardigan with vertical blue and yellow stripes, a light blue belt and a peach coloured taffeta underskirt. Most unusual of all were her blue, crepe-soled shoes.

The woman was wearing a cheap imitation wedding ring, stamped 'rolled gold' and, in Webster's estimation, had been dead for approximately eighteen months. Determining the cause of death proved problematic, since so little of the woman remained. Webster could find no trace of either natural illness or violence, apart from the fact that a piece of taffeta had been stuffed deep into her mouth; hence he drew the tentative conclusion that she had most probably been suffocated. The one thing of which he was absolutely certain was that the woman had been placed in the tree after her death. The widest internal measurement of the hollow trunk was 24in and it was too narrow for the woman to have climbed there herself.

An inquest was held at Stourbridge on 28 April and the coroner's jury returned a verdict of 'murder by some person or persons unknown' on the still unidentified remains.

The police were hampered in their investigations by the fact that the body had been discovered in the midst of the Second World War and the hostilities had considerably swelled the missing-persons lists. Nevertheless, they began an immediate search of the records, hunting for any missing person who matched the description of the remains found in the tree. They examined more than 3,000 reports of missing women, covering a geographical area of 1,000 miles^2. They also contacted clothing manufacturers and distributors, hoping to trace the garments that the woman had been wearing at the time of her death. Her shoes were particularly unusual and the police believed that they eventually managed to account for all but four pairs of the shoes that had ever been manufactured. Yet their efforts still did not produce any positive links to the identity of the mysterious woman.

Notices were posted in all of the main dental journals, seeking an identification of the woman's irregular dentition, but there was no response.

The only vague lead that the police had was a report from two men who had heard screams coming from within the wood in July 1941. At the time, the police had been called and an officer had searched the woods with the two men, although nothing unusual had been found. A group of gypsies had been camping in the area at the time and there was a record of police intervention in a minor domestic dispute – was the dead woman a member of the travelling fraternity?

With no firm leads, the police were forced to investigate some of the more bizarre theories put forward by members of the public, a number of whom had written to the local papers with the notion that the woman had been killed as part of a black magic ritual. Hagley Wood was rumoured to be the location of an active witches' coven and legend had it that the spirit of a witch could be successfully imprisoned in a hollow tree. In addition, the woman's hand had been severed and buried some distance away, a practice that has strong occult associations. A 'Hand of Glory', as such a severed hand was known, was believed to have the power to open locks, find hidden treasure and paralyse enemies.

The police were making little progress with their investigations when the first piece of graffiti appeared in the area. 'Who put Luebella down the which-elm?' was printed in chalk in neat capital letters on the wall of a building. The words 'Hagley Wood Bella' also appeared, as did 'Who put Bella in the wych elm?' Soon, the graffiti took on a standard format, 'Who put Bella down the wych elm – Hagley Wood?' and appeared regularly throughout the West Midlands. The police appealed for the writer or writers to come forward, but nobody ever did and, despite the fact that the messages were carefully and neatly printed in capital letters, which would have

REMAINS OF BODY
FOUND HERE
18 APRIL 1943

The old wych elm. (Courtesy of the Express and Star, *Wolverhampton)*

taken some time to execute, nobody ever saw the phantom writer at work. Those who favoured witchcraft as a solution to the mystery were quick to point out that the names Bella and Luebella – both derived from the name Elizabeth – had long associations with the black arts.

The police felt that whoever concealed the body of Bella in the trunk of the tree was most probably local and was thus aware of the tree's existence, since the fact that it was hollow wasn't readily apparent just by looking at it. They argued that a stranger to the area was unlikely to come across the tree by pure chance and would have been more likely to dispose of a body in the wood by burying it.

In 1945, Professor Webster was called upon to investigate a second murder, this time at Lower Quinton in Warwickshire, approximately 40 miles from Hagley. In this case, the victim was Charles Walton, a seventy-four-year-old villager who was murdered on St Valentine's Day. Walton's body was found close to a willow tree, pinned to the ground by his own pitchfork, which had been thrust through his throat with such force that it took two policemen to remove it. His throat had also been slashed with a billhook and the same weapon had been used to carve the sign of the cross on his chest.

Although Scotland Yard was called in to assist the local police with their enquiries, Walton's murder was never solved The only real clue to the murder – if indeed it was a clue – was a passage from an old book describing the method of murder as one that had been used in 1885 to kill a woman believed to have been a witch. Although suspicion for the murder fell on Walton's employer, his involvement was never proven and it was strongly believed by villagers at the time that Walton had either been killed as a ritual sacrifice to ensure plentiful crops or that he had been somehow connected with the occult and had been killed by someone who feared his magical powers. As with Hagley Bella, his death was recorded as 'murder by person or persons unknown'. Certainly, an eminent archaeologist of the time, Dr Margaret Murray, who was also a leading expert on the occult, believed that the two murders were connected and that 'devil worshippers' were responsible for committing both.

The case of Hagley Bella eventually went cold, the police having exhausted every possible avenue of enquiry without managing to even establish her true identity, yet alone that of her killer. However, in 1953, journalist Wilfred Byford-Jones wrote about the case under the pen name 'Quaestor' in the local newspaper, the *Express and Star*.

Renewed interest in the case prompted the writing of several letters to the newspaper by members of the public amongst which was one signed simply 'Anna'. Anna's letter dispelled any connections between Bella's murder and witchcraft, suggesting instead that Bella had been killed because she had known too much about a wartime spy ring operating in the area and was judged to be a danger to its members.

After several appeals, 'Anna' apparently agreed to a meeting with 'Quaestor', at which she told an incredible story about a group of pro-German conspirators at work in the Hagley area, whose members had included a Dutchman, a foreign trapeze artist and a British Officer, to whom Anna was related, who had died insane in 1942.

According to 'Quaestor', much of the information given to him by Anna was later verified, either by the police or by MI5. However, no arrests were made and the police released no further information about this particular branch of their enquiries to the public. Author Donald McCormick subsequently addressed the espionage angle in his book *Murder by Witchcraft*. McCormick believed that Bella was most probably a Dutch woman who supposedly parachuted into the area around Kidderminster in 1941 and subsequently vanished without trace.

The female spy, with the codename 'Clara', was thought to be a relative of Dutch spy Johannes Marius Dronkers, who was executed for treachery at Wandsworth Prison in 1942. Yet McCormick admitted that his theories were based on purely circumstantial evidence and that there was no way of proving them. However, if Bella were a foreigner, it would explain why the police were unable to trace her through the British missing persons lists and why no dentists responded to the appeals to identify her teeth.

Tantalisingly, Professor Webster, who retired due to ill health in 1955, made an appearance on television in 1958, in which he claimed that the police had

Wandsworth Prison, 1905. (Author's collection)

successfully identified the body. However, he refused to elaborate further on the matter, as did the police.

As well as connections with witchcraft and the wartime spy ring, other theories have revolved around the Romany gypsy encampment, known to have been in the area at around the time Bella died. Romanies are said to have their own traditional system of laws and justice and many believed that it was possible that Bella had been subjected to an impromptu trial and execution for some serious misdemeanour. Police dismissed this theory, saying that although the Romanies had been known to expel people from their families, they were not known for carrying out random executions. But, once again, if Bella were part of a travelling community, the inability of the police to identify her is explained.

Some believe that Bella was a local prostitute. Others are of the opinion that she was the random victim of a murderer who, so far at least, has been fortunate enough to evade detection. Some even talk of a conspiracy, believing that the police knew far more about the mystery than they were ever prepared to admit.

Several psychics have investigated the case of Hagley Bella over the years and the police have prided themselves on remaining open-minded and being prepared to consider any information, no matter from where it came. One psychic who was known to have visited the wych elm was George Elwell, who, in 1955, made a tape recording of himself allegedly in a trance at the site. Elwell positively identified Bella as a woman from Leeds named Annie Bradley and described her killer as a tall serviceman who sported a moustache. The police checked this information, but could find no missing person named Annie Bradley, from Leeds or anywhere else in the country.

In June 1964, there was a brief flurry of new interest in the case when a freshly dug grave was discovered by a forestry worker near to Bella's tree. However, when the 'body' was exhumed, it turned out to be the remains of a dog.

The familiar graffiti concerning Bella reappeared in the area in the mid-1980s, although this was believed to have been an attempt to create publicity for a pop song

Hagley Wood and Monument. (© N. Sly, 2008)

written about the case. Plays have been written about the mystery and, in 2003, an opera written by Simon Holt entitled *Who put Bella in the Wych Elm?* premiered at the Aldeburgh Festival.

Officially, the mystery of Hagley Bella remains unsolved and the West Mercia Police Force file on the case remains open to this day. The only things that are absolutely certain are that, in around 1941, somebody, somewhere in the world, lost a daughter, a sister, a mother or a female friend and that somebody, somewhere in the world, knew her identity and that of her murderer or murderers. More than sixty-five years later, it is likely that those who kept her secrets for so long took that knowledge to the grave.

23

'ARE YOU ALL RIGHT?'

Bromsgrove, 1944

The Second World War was an extremely busy time for the people of Bromsgrove and its surrounding area, as it was home to two hospitals that had been specifically created soon after the outbreak of the war to deal with casualties of the hostilities. One such hospital was situated at Norton Farm, on the Birmingham road, and was used for treating soldiers with neurological problems. In 1943, this collection of temporary huts was handed over to the American forces and the neurological unit was re-housed in a second nearby hospital, Barnsley Hall.

Barnsley Hall had opened in 1907 as the Bromsgrove Lunatic Asylum. Thirty new wards were built in its grounds at the start of the Second World War and it was quickly to become one of the largest emergency hospitals in the country, treating everyone from air-raid victims to front-line soldiers who had been invalided out of active service. Many of the patients had been seriously disfigured and they were encouraged to mingle with the local community at every possible opportunity.

Yet, while the people of Bromsgrove saw more than their fair share of tragedy and human suffering during the war years, they still managed to have some fun. There were endless dances, whist drives and concerts, all intended to raise money for the war effort. The American soldiers billeted throughout the area fully entered into the spirit of Worcestershire country life and were much appreciated by the local girls, who were drawn to their smart uniforms and film-star accents, previously only ever heard at the local cinemas. The Americans always seemed to have plenty of money, which they spent freely, and they also had access to some of the luxury items such as cigarettes, stockings and chocolate that had been so strictly rationed in England for several years. The Bromsgrove area provided several so-called 'GI Brides' and there were also a number of unmarried mothers; girls who were seduced by what seemed to be the promise of an exciting new life, only to be left high and dry when

Little Heath Lane, Lickey End. (© N. Sly, 2008)

their American lovers were quickly transferred out of the area as soon as their commanding officers found out about their affairs.

Florence 'Florrie' Porter lived with her family on Little Heath Lane at Lickey End and was in her thirties when the Americans first arrived in Bromsgrove. Her father had died some years earlier and she had two older sisters, both of whom had married and left home, as well as a younger brother who served in the Air Force.

Florrie was an intelligent woman who worked as a clerk in the wages office of the Austin Motor Co. at Longbridge, which, during the war years, produced an enormous range of essential items from ambulances to aeroplanes, as well as continuing to produce cars. She was a tall, statuesque woman who enjoyed music and dancing, at one time even playing in a local jazz band, but, by 1944, thirty-three-year-old Florrie devoted most of her free time to war work and had joined the St John Nursing Division at the Longbridge Works.

In spite of her busy life, Florrie still managed somehow to find the time to socialise and on 26 October 1944, she walked into Bromsgrove with her older sister, Doris, telling her that she had arranged to meet a man named Hal. (She had told her other sister, Winifred, about the meeting the day before.) Several people saw a woman believed to be Florrie in the smoke room of the George Hotel, in the company of an American officer and the couple were seen leaving the pub together at around ten minutes to ten. The officer was described as either a first or second lieutenant, aged between twenty-four and thirty years old. He was around 5ft 8in tall and was well built, with a bull neck. He had a low brow and dark hair, cut in what was known at the time as a 'combat crop', although the cut was beginning to grow out and his hair, which stuck up slightly, was sufficiently long to be brushed back from his forehead.

The Porter's next-door neighbour saw Florrie walking past the end of School Lane in Lickey End with the American officer at around twenty past ten that evening. Although he only saw the couple from the rear, it must be remembered that, at 5ft 10in, Florrie was unusually tall for a woman, a fact that made her quite easily recognisable, even from a distance. Her neighbour described the soldier as wearing a mackintosh blouse, dark trousers and a hat. Meanwhile, Florrie's mother was not unduly worried when her daughter didn't return home that night as Florrie often stayed the night with friends in Bromsgrove to save a long walk home in the dark and, as the night of 26 October was very wet and windy, her mother presumed that she had simply decided not to brave the foul weather.

Florrie was not seen again until early the following morning when two boys, ten-year-old Albert Egan and his friend Louis Price, aged seven, were cycling to school. As they passed the village school at Lickey End, Albert spotted something blue lying under a veranda in front of the building. When he stopped to investigate, he saw that the blue object that had caught his eye was the underwear worn by a woman, who was lying on her back in the school grounds. Thinking that she had simply fallen over, the two boys asked the woman, 'Are you all right?' When they got closer, it was all too obvious that she wasn't.

Albert sent Louis to fetch Mrs Parry, the school caretaker, who, after checking the boy's story, went to a neighbour, Mrs Smith, who had one of the few telephones

Lickey End School. (© N. Sly, 2008)

in the area at the time. Mrs Smith rang the police and four officers immediately responded to her call. As Louis and Albert had already discovered, the dead body of a woman lay beneath the veranda on her back, her head turned slightly to one side. There was a large pool of blood on the ground close to the body. The woman's skirt was pulled up around her waist, exposing the blue underwear that had caught Albert's attention as he cycled by. Her coat was undone and her gloves lay beside her head. Her clothing was torn, although her underwear appeared to be in place, and one of her shoes was missing, as was her handbag, if indeed she had been carrying one.

The school was closed for the day and the police called in pathologist Professor James Webster, who, after a number of photographs had been taken, supervised the removal of the body to the mortuary at Bromsgrove, where it was later identified as that of Florence Porter by her sister, Winnie. When Professor Webster performed a post-mortem examination, he found that Florrie had died from a combination of blood loss and shock, the result of multiple stab wounds, which had penetrated her throat, heart and lungs.

Her face was badly bruised, as if from being punched, and it appeared that she had initially been hit with such force that it had knocked her backwards, causing her to strike the back of her head on a hard surface such as a wall or the school playground. She had then been stabbed several times in her head and neck, with one stab wound puncturing the jugular vein and the carotid artery on the left-hand side of her throat. There were a further six stabs wounds in her chest, one of which had penetrated her heart. These had been made through the jumper she was wearing, which had holes corresponding to the knife wounds. Her clothing had been disturbed, but Professor Webster could find no evidence either of rape or of any other sexual activity, consensual or otherwise. Although there was blood under the fingernails of one hand, there were no cuts to her hands and arms, suggesting that she had been rendered unconscious by the impact to the back of her head before being stabbed, since she had obviously not tried to defend herself against her knife-wielding attacker.

With the assistance of a number of US Army Officers, the police organised a party of special constables and volunteers to assist them in conducting a search of the surrounding fields and gardens. They were hoping to find the murder weapon, thought by Professor Webster to be a knife with a half-inch wide blade, but what they eventually found was Florrie Porter's handbag, discarded in bushes in the garden of a private house, which lay roughly half a mile towards Bromsgrove from the school. In spite of the fact that the police had access to US Forces metal detectors, more usually used for locating landmines in war zones, and, even though local pools were drained, no trace of the murder weapon was ever found.

Interviews with people living close to the school brought forth the information that a woman's screams had been heard at about half-past ten on the night of the murder, but since the weather had been so atrocious at the time, nobody had taken much notice. School caretaker Mrs Parry told the police that the school gates were always locked at night, but that courting couples frequently gained entrance to the grounds by lifting the gates off their hinges.

The murder of Florrie Porter caused near panic among the women in the area, particularly as it occurred only a month after the murder of another woman with associations with Bromsgrove. Polish refugee Ruth Schmereler, aged twenty, had last been seen alive in Bromsgrove on 21 September, when she had set out from the area to hitchhike to Manchester. Her body had been found six days later in a disused quarry at Cheadle, Staffordshire. Like Florrie Porter, Ruth had been stabbed in the chest.

Police quickly issued a statement to say that, after careful investigation, they had reached the conclusion that the two murders were not connected in any way, but, even so, rumours that both had been committed by the same man persisted in the community and the female nightshift workers at the local factories insisted on waiting until daylight before they made their way home from work.

In spite of newspaper appeals for the American officer who had been seen with Florrie on the night of her death to come forward, perhaps not surprisingly, nobody ever did. The police also appealed for information from anyone who had given a lift to a soldier on 26 or 27 October, either British or American, but again, their appeals failed to elicit any response.

Florrie Porter. (Courtesy of Worcestershire News)

Mr F.P. Evers, the coroner for North Worcestershire, opened an inquest at Bromsgrove into Miss Porter's death. Initially opened immediately after the murder and adjourned to allow the police more time to conduct their enquiries, on 9 December 1944, the jury eventually returned a verdict of 'wilful murder by person or persons unknown.'

At first, the police were confident of their ability to solve the murder of Florrie Porter, believing that they had only to identify 'Hal', who was the most likely suspect. The police questioned a large number of Americans serving in the area and also arranged for those witnesses who had seen Florrie on the night of her death to attend the American bases, to see if they could pick out her companion. Potential witnesses attended many ID parades, walking along seemingly endless lines of American soldiers, with instructions to tap anyone that they recognised on the shoulder. However, the American officer was never identified.

Rumour and speculation abounded in the area and it was widely believed that Hal had been identified by his commanding officers and had been quickly transferred out of the area.

More than fifty years later, the police reviewed their files on the murder of Florrie Porter and tried to put an end to the rumours of a cover-up once and for all. They released a statement to say that they had found no evidence of anyone being spirited away in a hurry to avoid detection. At the time, the entire locality was flooded with American servicemen and, although there had initially been two strong suspects, both had given alibis for the time of the murder and both alibis had been rigorously checked and verified.

In February 2006, the murder was covered by the BBC's *Inside Out* programme, which followed the progress of a distant relative of Miss Porter, who has been conducting her own investigations into the case. The programme featured an interview with the son of one of the original witnesses, the barmaid at the George Hotel, Annie Richardson. He believed that his mother actually did recognise the man at an identity parade, but was too afraid to tell the police after her family was threatened.

If the murderer was indeed one of the two strong suspects identified by the police at the time of Miss Porter's death, it appears as if somebody went to a lot of trouble to protect him, first agreeing to provide and confirm a false alibi, then using threats of violence against a potential witness who might identify the killer. Meanwhile, amidst persistent allegations of a cover-up and of information deliberately being withheld, the West Mercia Police file on the killing of Florence Porter remains open and, at the time of writing, the murder remains officially unsolved.

24

'I WANT TO SAY IT WAS A SUDDEN URGE'

On 12 May 1958, nine-year-old Leonard William Hall of Eddy Road, Kidderminster didn't go to school but instead spent the afternoon playing outside with some of his seven brothers and sisters. During the course of the afternoon, his mother, Nellie, noticed that he was no longer with his siblings, but she wasn't unduly worried as Leonard often went off to play with his friends. However, the boy didn't return for his tea and, as the evening progressed with no sign of Leonard, she grew ever more anxious.

When Leonard still hadn't come home by the time his father arrived home from his work as a farm labourer at ten o'clock that night, Mrs Hall was almost frantic with worry. At her insistence, Leonard's father – also called Leonard – went straight to the police station to report his son missing. However, Mr Hall's arrival at the police station didn't prompt an immediate search for his son as he had hoped. Sadly, by then, the police were all too aware of young Leonard's whereabouts and the news they had for his father was the worst that he could possibly imagine.

At seven o'clock that evening, Gordon Broome and Michael Gale, both aged nine, had been playing on a piece of wasteland when they had spotted a boy lying on the grass beneath a hawthorn hedge at the bottom of a slope. They couldn't make up their minds whether the boy was asleep or dead and, after a few minutes discussion, they decided that they had better go and find a 'grown-up'.

The first adults they saw were railway fireman Jesse Cooke and his wife, who were walking across the new market site at Hoo Road when the boys ran up to them. Cooke took one look at the 'sleeping' child then rushed to the nearest telephone box to call the police.

Eddy Road, Kidderminster. (© N. Sly, 2008)

The police sped to the scene. The wasteland was a desolate place, on the side of a hill, which was overgrown with brambles and hawthorn trees. The boy lay on the grass, naked from the waist down, with the exception of a pair of grey socks that had been put on inside out and brown leather shoes. He wore a greenish-yellow knitted sweater over a blue-striped short-sleeved shirt and his trousers and underpants were draped over a bush a few feet from his body. His trouser pockets contained a torch case and a plastic toy boat and around his body lay a number of old music sheets, one of which had been fashioned into the shape of a dart and lay beneath the child's body.

Leonard Hall senior was taken to the site from the police station, where he immediately realised that the search for his missing son was over before it had even begun.

The boy's body was photographed by police photographers and examined where it lay by pathologist Dr Albert Charles Hunt, a lecturer in forensic pathology at the University of Bristol, who was also attached to the Home Office Forensic Science Laboratory in Birmingham. Hunt carried out a post-mortem examination on the boy's body in the early hours of the morning of 13 May. He determined that Leonard had died due to manual strangulation and that he had been violated either just before or immediately after his death.

The child's body was covered with scratches, some of which appeared to have been made by brambles, others on his chest, abdomen and upper thighs being more consistent with human fingernails. Hunt tried to take scrapings from beneath Leonard's fingernails, but they were bitten to the quick. In examining the boy's clothes, he noted seven small spots of blood on the front of the child's shirt and was of the opinion that they did not come from any of the child's injuries.

The police immediately began investigations into the child's murder, calling in police from New Scotland Yard to help with their enquiries. Straight away, they began to receive reports that Leonard had been seen in the company of a man on the afternoon of 12 May. Armed with a description of the man, who was said to have distinctive ginger hair, the police began knocking on doors and, at one o'clock in the morning, they reached Queen Street and spoke to a lodger there, Alfred Gwynne.

Gwynne was asleep in bed when the police arrived. The thirty-six-year-old man worked as a labourer and had lived in Kidderminster for most of his life. When Detective Inspector Rex Jones arrived at his lodgings to interview him, he asked him if he would mind getting up and getting dressed. When Gwynne came downstairs, Jones noticed that he was wearing three pairs of trousers, two made from flannel and one made from khaki denim. In answer to Jones's question, Gwynne assured him that he was wearing the same clothes on the previous day and that they were all the clothes he had, apart from a leather jacket and his fawn mackintosh, which he had left lying on the foot of his bed.

Gwynne bore a resemblance to descriptions of the man seen with Leonard. He was told that the police were investigating a serious offence in Kidderminster and was invited to go to the police station to give an account of his movements on the previous afternoon. He agreed without hesitation.

He told the police that he had been at the Roadhouse Café in Kidderminster until a quarter to three, when he had walked to the Central Cinema and watched

Queen Street, Kidderminster. (© N. Sly, 2008)

Bull Ring, Kidderminster, 1950s. (Author's collection)

the latest Elvis Presley film, *Jailhouse Rock*. However, he had not enjoyed the film at all, so had left the cinema at about five o'clock, before the film had finished, and gone to the Bull Ring Café.

He admitted that he had been with a boy that afternoon, but only briefly – as he was leaving the Roadhouse, a boy of about four or five years old had run into him outside. Gwynne described the child as '...looking as if he had been playing in the muck' and said that he had told him that he couldn't go into the café looking like that. However, the boy had ignored him and run into the café.

While Gwynne was being questioned at the police station, it was noticed that he had a fresh scratch on the back of his hand and a scab on his thumb. He consented to his hands being photographed and also to being examined by Dr Hunt, who pointed out some small spots of blood on Gwynne's mackintosh. Gwynne said that the coat had been 'pinched' and did not belong to him, although he admitted that the blood was his, from the scratch on his hand, which he said had been made by the cat in the Roadhouse Café.

Having given his statement, Gwynne was allowed to leave the police station, but, as reports from the public continued to come in, it quickly became obvious that he was a prime suspect in the murder. Several people who actually knew both Gwynne and Leonard contacted the police to say that they had seen them together.

One of these was park keeper Mr John Henry Wilkes, who had seen Leonard and Gwynne together in St George's Park at about 3.15 p.m. Wilkes knew Leonard well, having had occasion to take his name and address in the past after a few childish pranks. As Wilkes watched, Leonard and Gwynne went into the gent's toilet in the park together. He followed them and, when Leonard ran out of the toilet, he asked him why he wasn't at school.

Wilkes later saw the man and boy leaving the park by the Waterloo Street exit, where they were also seen by Mr Stubley, who ran a marine store in Waterloo Street. Stubley knew Gwynne, but did not know the little boy who accompanied him. The man and boy had walked off together in the direction of Coventry Street.

Gwynne and Leonard were next seen by a group of schoolgirls who were walking in line to their swimming lesson. One of the girls, Kathleen Stewart, knew Gwynne and another, Mary Howe, knew Leonard, who often played with her brothers and sisters. By now, Gwynne and Leonard were on the steps leading up to a white house on the hill near J.H. Smith's builder's yard, less than 70 yards from where Leonard's body was to be discovered just hours later.

In the light of statements received from several witnesses, the police spoke to the staff at the Central Cinema. Mrs Clarice Southall, who worked in the confectionery kiosk, lived in the same street as Gwynne and had known him for about five years. She told the police that she had not seen him come into the cinema on 12 May, adding that if he had come in from two o'clock onwards, he could not have got in without her seeing him.

Cinema manager, Victor Sims, told the police that *Jailhouse Rock* had been showing at the Central, starting on 12 May, and that it had previously been shown in other Midlands towns, including Leamington, where Gwynne had been working until the Friday night before the murder. On 12 May the programme started at 1.50 p.m., with the main feature beginning at 2.07 p.m. and ending at 3.43 p.m. Gwynne had told the police that he had left the cinema in the middle of the film, immediately after a scene in which Presley was shown hitting a warder. Sims told the police that this particular scene would have been screened between 2.27 p.m. and 2.28 p.m. and would not have been shown again until 5.39 p.m. during the evening performance.

Gwynne was called back to the police station for further questioning and continued to deny having been to any of the places where witnesses had told the police they had seen him. He also denied being in the company of a small boy, apart from the brief encounter outside the café. On 15 May, Detective Superintendent Joseph Kennedy from New Scotland Yard told Gwynne, 'I don't think you are telling the truth,' and informed him that the police were planning to place him in an identification parade.

'I will have the identification,' said Gwynne defiantly. 'It was all true what I said in my sheet.'

Moments later, he admitted that he had been in the park and the toilet on 12 May, but insisted he had not been with a little boy. Kennedy told him that he had also been seen going up the steps by the new market site with a boy.

High Street, Kidderminster. (Author's collection)

'The steps?' echoed Gwynne. 'I haven't been up there since the firm knocked off at the site the other week.' Gwynne then paused for a minute or two before telling the police officer, 'I can't figure things out half the time. I can't just think. You may think I'm pulling your leg. Maybe I did do it but I cannot explain. I admit I didn't go to the pictures.'

Kennedy left the room to attend the inquest into Leonard's death, telling Gwynne that he would be put up for identification at midday. His clothes were taken away and he was given different ones to wear at the identity parade. As Gwynne was changing his clothes, he suddenly dissolved into tears. 'I would like to speak to Mr Kennedy,' he told Detective Sergeant MacMillan. 'I want to tell him it was just a sudden urge.'

'I want to say it was a sudden urge. It's all true. I killed him,' Gwynne told Kennedy when he came back to the interview room. He then burst into tears again and went on to make a full confession to the murder of Leonard Hall. 'I took him up the steps like they said. I don't know what came over me.'

Gwynne was brought before magistrates at Kidderminster on 18 and 19 June, charged with murdering Leonard Hall. Mr E.G. MacDermott, for the Director of Public Prosecutions, first outlined the facts of the case then called a series of witnesses, many of whom had seen Leonard Hall in the company of Alfred Gwynne on 12 May. Both Mr and Mrs Hall appeared in court, where Mr Hall admitted that he had known Gwynne for several years. He described being taken to the Hoo Road site to identify his son's body, pointing at Gwynne in court and saying, 'and that's the bloke who done it over there.'

Next, pathologist Albert Hunt described his initial and post-mortem examinations of the boy's body, telling the court that Leonard had died as a result of pressure to his neck from something broad, such as a man's forearm or hands. Whoever had killed the child would have needed to exert that pressure for at least half a minute and maybe even for several minutes.

The police related their various interviews with Gwynne, both before and after his eventual arrest, and cinema manager Victor Sims confirmed that Gwynne's account of the film *Jailhouse Rock* didn't concur with the actual times at which the film was being shown.

The second day of the proceedings opened with more evidence from the police. John Merchant, of the West Midland Forensic Science Laboratory, who had examined various items for the police, followed them into the witness box. Both Gwynne and Leonard Hall were blood group O, which, not surprisingly, was the group of the blood found on Hall's shirt and on the paper dart beneath his body. It was also the same group as the stains on Gwynne's raincoat. However, wool fibres found beneath Gwynne's fingernails were identical to those from the socks that Leonard was wearing when he was discovered and couldn't have come from any of the garments that Gwynne was wearing. In addition, a single, fresh hawthorn blossom was found in the pocket of Gwynne's raincoat, similar to the flowering hawthorn near where the body had been found

Finally, Gwynne's confession was discussed, with the police assuring the court that it had been made voluntarily and that they were absolutely sure that Gwynne knew exactly what he was saying when he made it.

Having heard all the evidence, magistrates Mr James Ferguson, Mrs S. Stone and Mr Derek Woodward committed Gwynne to stand trial at the next assizes. The counsel for the prosecution pushed for the case to be tried at Stafford but Mr Savery, who was defending Gwynne, objected that this would not give him much time to formulate his defence. Eventually, it was agreed that the case would go to Birmingham Assizes in July 1958. Savery then asked the magistrates for a second defence counsel, in view of the gravity of the case, but his request was turned down.

In the event, the legal arguing that took place after Gwynne's appearance before the magistrates was completely irrelevant. His trial for the murder of Leonard William Hall opened on 15 July 1958 before Mr Justice Streatfeild and Gwynne pleaded 'Guilty'. Thus, there was no formal trial, just a mandatory sentence of life imprisonment handed down by the judge.

25

'YOU'LL GET THE SAME DOSE AS YOUR MATE WHEN YOU COME OUT'

Worcester, 1961

The sight of a man staggering along a road late on a Saturday night is not an uncommon one in most cities and, on 8 April 1961, people studiously ignored the young man stumbling along Commandery Road in Worcester, assuming that he was simply inebriated. However, when the man eventually collapsed on a footpath in Sidbury, two young men went to his aid and found that he was not drunk but bleeding heavily from a wound in his chest. The police and an ambulance were called, with Sergeant Arthur Tyler being the first to arrive and rendering what first aid he could, trying his hardest to stem the constant flow of blood from the man's chest. At 11.57 p.m. the man was admitted to the casualty department of the Worcester Royal Infirmary. Unfortunately, doctors there barely had a chance to start treating him, as he died just after midnight, without having regained consciousness.

The deceased man was quickly identified as twenty-two-year-old Irish labourer Patrick Mulligan, who lodged with his sister at Hamilton Road, Worcester. From the scene of his collapse, the police were able to follow a trail of his blood back to the public toilets at Commandery Road, where it appeared that Mulligan had been stabbed. A post-mortem examination, conducted by Dr Albert Hunt, showed that the cause of his death had been a single stab wound, which had penetrated the right-hand side of his heart. It had been inflicted with a sharp instrument, such as a knife, which had a blade that was roughly 3in in length and sharp on both edges

Commandery Road, Worcester. (© N. Sly, 2008)

and which Hunt believed was most probably a dagger. There was a second cut 2½in below the fatal wound, although this was just a fairly minor flesh wound. Hunt also estimated that, shortly before his death, Mulligan had consumed the equivalent of six pints of beer or 9⅔oz of spirits.

Within hours of the killing, police arrested three demolition workers from Birmingham and charged them with the murder. Robert Reid, aged twenty-eight, Joseph Culloty, aged twenty-four and eighteen-year-old Robert Jayes were brought before magistrates and remanded in custody to allow the police more time to complete their enquiries. All three men denied any knowledge of the murder.

Meanwhile, the police issued an urgent appeal to the public to try and trace a man seen near the public toilets at around the time that Mulligan was stabbed. Said to be about fifty years old, the man was 6ft tall and believed to be a tramp. He was clean-shaven and wore a full-length overcoat over another coat. He also wore a cap and carried a bag similar to those used to carry gas masks during the Second World War. The police stressed that the tramp was not a suspect, although they believed that he could assist them in their enquiries.

Curiously, the tramp was also thought to have carried a rather distinctive cushion, which the police had found in the public toilets. Described as being home-made from green and yellow tartan, the cushion was stuffed with flock and had been hand-sewn with turquoise thread around the edges. The police appealed for anyone to come forward who had either lost such a cushion, or had seen a man with the cushion in his possession.

Describing the hunt for the tramp as a nationwide search, Mr Eric Abbott, the Chief Constable of Worcester, stated that he had called in Scotland Yard to assist in his enquiries and Detective Superintendent Hawkins of the Murder Squad subsequently arrived in Worcester from London a few days after the murder. Abbott told newspapers that he also wished to speak to anyone who had been in Sidbury or High Street between eleven o'clock and midnight, especially a ginger-haired youth who was seen on a bicycle in Commandery Road around the time of the murder. The Chief Constable also appealed to people in the area to search their gardens for the murder weapon, asking them to pay particular attention to cellars with street level gratings. Finally, they appealed for the identity of a young man who had assisted the dying man before driving off in a cream or fawn coloured car, which was believed to be either a Ford Anglia saloon, a Consul or a Zephyr.

The three men who had been arrested in connection with the murder made another appearance before magistrates on 18 April. Then, the case took a dramatic turn when Mr David Prys Jones addressed the court at the opening of the proceedings. Acting for the Director of Public Prosecutions, Prys Jones asked for the charge of murder against the three defendants to be withdrawn.

He described the murder on 8 April and the arrest of the three men on the following day. Stating that, at the time, the police had sufficient reason to arrest and charge the three men, he informed the magistrates that enquiries made since the arrests had brought forth new information and, after all the evidence was made available to the Director of Public Prosecutions, he considered that it would be wrong to proceed with the murder charge against Reid, Culloty and Jayes. Prys Jones was understandably reticent to reveal exactly what new evidence had brought about this change of heart.

Robert Jayes was immediately discharged, while Robert Reid and Joseph Culloty were further charged with an assault on a Mr Ronald Hill in Worcester on 8 or 9 April. Both men pleaded guilty to assaulting Mr Hill and were each fined £50. After their dismissal from court, the local newspaper spoke to Robert Jayes, who told them that he had spent his remand in Gloucester Prison 'reading books and comics and thinking'. Culloty simply said, 'It's great to be free.' The mistakenly accused men were all said to be considering proceedings against the police for wrongful arrest.

With the discharge of the only three suspects to date in the murder case, the police intensified their search for the murder weapon, deciding to drain a large section of the Worcester-Birmingham Canal, near to Sidbury Bridge. The Worcestershire Fire Brigade was called in and six portable pumps were set up, each capable of draining 300 gallons of water per minute. Their first attempt was unsuccessful when, having almost completed the task, a makeshift dam gave way and instantly refilled the newly drained stretch of canal.

On their second attempt, the police permanently positioned two men at the dam to make sure that it remained intact. At two o'clock in the morning, when the canal was all but drained, a large crack appeared in the dam and the water immediately began to pour back into the canal. The men quickly breached the crack in the dam with sandbags, managing to halt the flow of water and, on the following morning, workers from British Waterways reinforced the structure with

Birmingham Canal at Worcester. (© N. Sly, 2008)

planks and yet more sandbags. They also rescued thousands of fish as the water level in the canal gradually fell, until just a few shallow pools remained.

In spite of torrential rain during the night, which had replaced several gallons of water, the canal was finally emptied of more than a million gallons of water and the muddy bottom was thoroughly searched by policemen in waders, each officer tethered by a rope to another officer on the canal banks. Raking through the silt with long forks, they found numerous bricks, old car tyres, discarded prams and other debris, but no knife was found.

Even though the search of the canal had disappointing results, the police had now traced the owner of the tartan cushion, who came forward as a result of a televised appeal. They were also inundated with possible sightings of the tramp, from all over the country. On 23 April, they trawled condemned houses and farm buildings in the Worcester area, questioning anybody they found sleeping rough and also interrupted the showing of films at cinemas throughout the Midlands by displaying an identikit picture of the wanted man on the screens.

An arrest was made in London on 10 May 1961, after a man appeared at Mansion House Court on a charge of begging. As he had already been in custody for a day prior to his court hearing, the man's sentence of one day's imprisonment for his offence meant his immediate release at the conclusion of his hearing. Waiting for him were Chief Inspector William Paterson of the Worcester Police and Detective Superintendent Denis Hawkins of Scotland Yard, who informed him that he was being charged with the murder of Patrick Mulligan in Worcester on 8 April.

Clifford Newsam, an unemployed marine engineer of no fixed abode, denied any knowledge of, or involvement in, the murder, although he was said to bear a strong resemblance to a man seen in the public lavatory shortly before Mulligan's death. On his arrest he told Paterson, 'Well, I would just like to say, sir, that I am not guilty. I have never been to Worcester in my life before.' Nevertheless, the thirty-nine-year-old man was immediately taken to Worcester, where he appeared before magistrates and was remanded in custody.

By his second appearance before the magistrates, on 18 May, Newsam had been granted legal aid for his defence and his solicitor, Mr Hugh McNaught, shocked the magistrates by applying for bail. McNaught said that he realised that it was a most unusual request, since bail was very rarely granted for an accused charged with murder, but he described his client as being in 'a hopeless position'. Newsam had been arrested following the publication of identikit pictures, which McNaught described as 'pictures built up with an American contraption.'

The police had previously been seeking a fifty-year-old man who was at least 6ft tall – Newsam was thirty-nine and considerably shorter and continued to insist that he had never even been to Worcester, yet alone murdered someone there. He was willing to have a photograph of himself published in any medium, so that anyone who could prove otherwise would come forward or, better still, anyone who could support his alibi that he was in London at the time of the murder. This was, said McNaught, an enormous risk, since all the prosecution would need to do was to prove that Newsam was in Worcester at the relevant time and place and widespread publication of his picture might well jog some memories.

Newsam himself believed that he could find witnesses who could support his alibi for the time of the murder but he did not know their names – all he could do to defend himself was to visit them and ask them to contact the police, something he obviously could not do if he was incarcerated.

On behalf of the Worcester Police, Superintendent Joseph Davidson strongly opposed the solicitor's request for bail on the grounds of the seriousness of the charge against Newsam. In addition, as Newsam was of no fixed abode, the police could not be sure that he would not abscond if he were released on bail. The magistrates supported the objection and, having refused the application for bail, remanded Newsam in custody until 25 May.

Newsam was eventually to appear at Worcester Magistrates Court, accused of Mulligan's murder, in a hearing lasting for three days. Almost thirty witnesses were called over the three-day period, creating what McNaught referred to as 'the most amazing mass of contradictory evidence that has ever been put before a court.'

David Prys Jones opened the proceedings by describing the last night of Mulligan's life. He had been drinking with friends until around eleven o'clock, when he had left them, apparently intending to go home to his lodgings. He was seen at half-past eleven staggering across a road in Sidbury, eventually collapsing in the gutter.

One of Mulligan's drinking companions, a lifelong friend, John Kiernan, told the court that he and the deceased had visited two pubs together on the night of

Mulligan's death. Kiernan had met Mulligan in the street and together they had gone first to the Five Ways Hotel, where they had each drunk a pint of beer, then to the Fountain Inn, where they had drunk four more pints. At that time, Mulligan was behaving quietly and did not appear to be drunk.

They had left the Fountain Inn at closing time at ten o'clock and, as they left, Mulligan had engaged in a brief argument with a Scottish man, appearing to object to his singing. The argument had been confined to words only and Kiernan had swiftly hustled Mulligan away to avoid any trouble. Kiernan had got a taxi at half-past ten and had asked Mulligan, who often stayed with him on weekends, to come with him. However Mulligan had declined the invitation and Kiernan had last seen him walking off towards the town centre.

The prosecution then called Alexander Kennedy, the first of two long-distance lorry drivers who had visited the public conveniences in Commandery Road on the night of the murder.

Kennedy told the court that he was employed by British Road Services and that, on the night in question, had been driving a load from Bristol to Glasgow. He had stopped at the toilets at about ten past eleven on the night of 8 April. There was another lorry already parked outside the toilets and Kennedy chatted briefly to the driver, Edmund Ridley, before going into the public convenience.

One of the cubicle doors inside was shut and, according to Kennedy, a young, dark-haired man was kicking on the door shouting, 'Come out!' The man appeared to be drunk and, as Kennedy watched, he had taken several running kicks at the toilet door. Eventually, the cubicle door opened and the occupant came out and began arguing with the young man, at which point Kennedy went into the now vacant cubicle and shut the door. Inside, on the floor, was the yellow tartan cushion. He heard the man from the cubicle saying to the young man, 'you cannot use the toilet now, you foreign *******,' after which came the sound of a blow being struck and a high pitched voice shouting, 'I'll carve your guts out, you Irish *******.'

There followed a brief scuffle, after which both men ran out of the toilets. Seconds later, one returned and banged on the door of the cubicle occupied by Mr Kennedy, threatening, 'You'll get the same dose as your mate when you come out.'

Kennedy replied that the man was no mate of his and that he had a lorry outside and a job to do. At that point, Edmund Ridley entered the toilets and asked Kennedy if he was all right. Kennedy left his cubicle to see the man who had earlier occupied it putting something into his bag, which resembled a gas mask case. 'I'm sorry about that, Jock,' the man apologised to Kennedy, telling him that the Irishman had just stabbed him in the leg and run away. Kennedy noticed that the man's hand was bleeding and he was shaking it, so that drops of blood fell onto the toilet floor. The man had blood oozing from the side of his mouth and a sizeable patch of fresh blood on his coat, just above his right knee. Kennedy asked the man if the cushion belonged to him and the man said that it did.

Asked if he could identify the man in court, Kennedy immediately pointed out Clifford Newsam. Ridley confirmed Kennedy's account of the encounter and also pointed out Newsam as the man he had seen in the public toilets. While waiting for Kennedy to come out of the cubicle, Ridley had seen the man reflected in a mirror, holding what he believed was a knife.

Other witnesses were called who, having seen Newsam's photograph in the local papers, believed that they too had seen him in Worcester. One witness said that Newsam had begged food from her on 7 April and that she had given him some bread and butter. She particularly recalled the date as it was the second anniversary of a death. Another witness, Mrs Elizabeth Smith, testified to seeing Newsam close to the Commandery Road toilets, although she couldn't be sure if her sighting had been on the morning of the day of the murder or two days later.

James Barrett recognised Newsam's photograph as that of a man who had caused a drunken disturbance in a Worcester public house in either August or September of 1960. Barrett also said that he had seen the man again two days later, walking towards the Severn Bridge.

The magistrate's court was then given a full account of Clifford Newsam's known movements immediately before and after the murder. Between 26 March and 4 April, he had been employed as a plateman at Simpson's restaurant at the Strand in London but was fired after a dispute. On 4 April, he had been issued with a War Disability Pension voucher, which he had cashed in person at the London Cheapside branch of the Yorkshire Bank on 7 April. Both Mr Keith Faraday and Mr Henry Pennington, the bank's chief clerk and branch manager, testified to seeing Newsam in the bank on that day, both stating that his next visit to the bank had been on 10 April.

As Newsam was homeless, he had been sleeping in the Salvation Army Hostel at Waterloo Road, in London. Having lost his job, he still had three day's tickets for a bed left and Mr Thomas Perrin, the Salvation Army officer in charge of the hostel, confirmed that Newsam had slept there from 5 March to 6 April inclusive.

After that, Newsam told police that he had slept rough at either Waterloo or Liverpool Street stations. He admitted to drawing his £10 pension after being sacked from work, saying that he then went 'on the beer'.

Newsam's clothes had been sent for analysis to the West Midlands Forensic Laboratory at Birmingham, along with the tartan cushion. The senior analyst, Mr John Merchant testified that he had found nothing of significance on either the clothes or the cushion and that an examination of Newsam's fingernails and hair had revealed nothing to connect him to Mulligan's murder. There had been no blood found on any items of his clothing. Both Mulligan and Newsam were blood group O, the most common of all blood groups, so it was impossible to state that the blood found on the floor of the toilet was Newsam's blood. Newsam had no sign of any injury to his mouth and certainly no evidence of a stab wound on his leg. Furthermore, there were no bruises or other injuries to suggest that Newsam had recently been involved in a fight.

It was the contention of the prosecution that Clifford Newsam had travelled to Worcester from London, committed the murder and then returned to London again.

He had not been seen in London on either 8 or 9 April, thus giving him sufficient time to kill Mulligan in Worcester. Meanwhile, the counsel for the defence continued to insist that his client had never been to Worcester in his life before, questioning how a description of a 6ft tramp aged fifty as the man who had been fighting in the public toilets could possibly apply to his much younger and much shorter client.

Nevertheless, in spite of the conflicting evidence, Clifford Newsam was eventually committed by the magistrates to stand trial for the murder of Patrick Mulligan at the next Assizes in Stafford. However, the trial effectively collapsed when the counsel for the defence called a senior transport policeman, who testified to having seen Newsam at a railway station many miles from Worcester at the time of the murder. Newsam was subsequently acquitted.

Nobody else was ever charged with killing Patrick Mulligan and, at the time of writing, his murder remains unsolved.

BIBLIOGRAPHY & REFERENCES

BOOKS

Bradford, Anne, *Foul Deeds and Suspicious Deaths Around Worcester*, Barnsley, Wharncliffe Local History, 2008

Eddleston, John J., *The Encyclopaedia of Executions*, London, John Blake, 2004

Fielding, Steve, *The Hangman's Record Volume One 1868–1899*, Beckenham, Chancery Press, 1994

McCormick, Donald, *Murder by Witchcraft*, Arrow, 1969

NEWSPAPERS

Berrow's Worcester Journal
Express and Star, Wolverhampton
Kidderminster Shuttle
Stourport Courier and Worcestershire Mercury
The Times
Worcester News
Worcester News and Times

MAGAZINES

Murder Casebook, Volume 71, 1991. Ritual Killings London, Marshall Cavendish

DVD

Inside Out, Series 9, Programme 6, BBC Birmingham

Certain websites have also been consulted in the compilation of this book, but since they have a habit of disappearing, to avoid frustration, they have not been cited.

INDEX